Suffering in Silence

Angie & Danielle,
Il hope you enjoy
my book. Thanks

www.markleeowen.com

By Mark Owen

Suffering In Silence;
By Mark Owen

www.markleeowen.com
info@markleeowen.com

Cover design by www.royceowen.com
Published by www.markleeowen.com
Yakima, Washington

The locations are generalized and names of the people described in this book have been changed to protect privacy.

First Printing April 2005
Printed in Wyoming

ISBN 1-4116-2754-7

Contents

Dedication

My life trials, tribulations, newfound hope and inspiration, through the grace of God, are dedicated to my parents Brad and Linda Owen and Nancy and Terry Steinkamp. My brothers Adam and Royce, and my Sisters, Shanie, Dana and Sherri.

Preface

Although the names have been changed and the detail of specific events have been generalized, the revelation and willingness to face my personal trauma associated with my childhood abandonment, is written for you in hopes that you find the strength to embark on a life changing process of recovery, and freedom from the trauma that possess your own life. I hope that you find strength to peel away the layers of misplaced anger in your life, only to reveal the cause of your true emotional pain. I hope that you take the time to develop new life skills that will better enable you to cope with your feelings. I hope that you allow yourself the time to heal and process feelings so you'll never have to negatively react to life's challenges or self-medicate your pains again. I hope that you find a support base that inspires you to learn to share, communicate, trust, love and opens your minds and hearts to accept the reflection of the person that you really are, the innocent child born into this world by the parents that love you more than life itself.

I hope this process opens the channels of communication between yourself and your loved ones. I hope it challenges those around you to stop for a day and look beyond your guarded smile. I hope it challenges those that can provide support to look into your painful eyes and feel your broken heart. I pray that it encourages those that can do more to commit to provide resources for the life changing process we are about to embark upon.

I pray that my heart that's been opened for you, as detailed in the following pages, provides to you hope and inspiration that we no longer have to suffer in silence.

With Much Love,

Mark Lee Owen

Introduction

This is a story of a little boy abandoned by his biological family and left on the police station steps in Seoul, Korea when he was two and a half years old. With nothing more than a backpack, a Korean Bible, Korean rubber shoes and a story book, he was taken to White Lilly Orphanage, given a name and birth date. His adoption, like his life, almost didn't happen, as the director for Korean adoptions was embezzling funds to finance his senate campaign. After nine long months of waiting, a miraculous phone call was made. Despite the objections by the Korean government, his adoption through Holt International was approved.

By way of irreconcilable differences, his adopted parents were later divorced. His adopted father remarried and has since been elected Lieutenant Governor of the State of Washington. He is also the founder and president of a substance abuse prevention and anti bullying program. His adopted mother moved the family to Hawaii, where he spent the next six years with them as missionaries for Youth With A Mission (YWAM), a worldwide Christian training and outreach organization. She has since been' re-married and is the founder and president of an adoption agency that has offices located throughout the world. During his mother's evangelical pursuit, Mark traveled 13-European countries, and five in Asia. He was recognized in the *International Gymnast Magazine*, participated for a walk on role in a Japanese movie, and photo shoot for a local photography store.

He graduated Magna Cum Laude from Saint Martins College with a baccalaureate in accounting. He fostered a nine-year career chasing white-collar crime as a forensic accountant for the Washington State Auditors Office. He also served as the liaison between the state auditors office and the Department of Housing and Urban Development, Department of Agriculture for rural grants, Association of Washington Housing Authorities and the Washington Housing Administrative and Accounting Professionals. He was simultaneously creating a financial consulting firm where he had several contracts with the State's largest house banked casino and nonprofit organizations. Mark was on track to financial independence.

Despite his professional accomplishments, he was plagued with posttraumatic stress disorder from his abandonment as a child that was re-enforced when his adopted family divorced, his best friend committed suicide, and he lost his own child.

Mark had a secret life where he medicated these internal pains through alcohol, drugs, gambling and crime. These outlets led to his collapse that cost him his career, consulting firm, house, five totaled cars and any hope of having his own family.

Suffering In Silence; By Mark Owen is a true story of the hidden pains that physically, emotionally, mentally and spiritually bankrupted Mark.

Mark has emerged to share his story with others in hope that they no longer have to suffer in silence.

I

Adoption

Dear Mark,

    Why adoption? From the time I was little I always felt I was going to have 6 children and I had three little girls. I remember even in high school doing a project for orphaned children that really touched me. In the 70's, when the United States was pulling out of Viet Nam, just seeing all the orphans really tugged at my heart. I did some research locally to check into the adoption process. All the agencies said that it would take about 10-years. That was pretty discouraging. I remember talking with a friend of ours about the lengthy waiting period. However, she informed me that she had been checking into adoption as well. She told me of a place she had located to try to adopt a child from Viet Nam. I'd been seeing all the news stories about the children in the orphanages, and the relief organizations trying to get some of the children out before the communists took over. So I contacted the same agency.

They told me that they already had families for all the Vietnamese children. However, they also had children from Korea, "would we be interested in Korea?" I'd never thought of Korea, but where the child came from wasn't an issue, it was the child that was important to me. They sent the paperwork and I filled it out, and we sent it in. It felt really weird filling out paperwork for a child, especially having to say what sex, age range and type of child. It made me feel like I was buying a car instead of having a son or daughter! It almost made me physically sick to my stomach that something so important was reduced to paperwork, but that is how the process works.

Since the adoption agency was located out of the State of Washington, we had to research to find a person qualified to perform a home study and approve our home for you to live. I was able to get a social worker from the State of Washington to come and try. She had never done an international adoption before, but was willing to do ours. She visited the home and interviewed us, then we had to spend several months getting approval from the United States Immigration to bring a child into the United States, this in addition to the many other documents we had to gather. Finally, all the documentation was sent to Korea. We waited for them to match a child with our request.

I remember the day when the social worker called and said to come to her office; she had pictures of a little boy for us! As far as I was concerned, we could not get to that office fast enough!! I can't remember the exact date, but I think it was the end of October, or early November. She showed us two little black and white pictures of you, told us your estimated age, and that you were found on the police station steps in Seoul, Korea. She asked if we wanted you! My gosh, did we want you!?! Of course!!! There was not even a hesitation! In the pictures you looked so sad, it broke my heart. How soon would you be able to come was all I cared about.

Then there was some kind of problem in Korea with an official from the orphanage and they stopped releasing any of the children to come the United States. We learned the Korean Director had been using the money that was being sent to help the children, for his political campaign for the Korean Senate. It was discovered and he was being investigated by the Korean government. Some of the people from the United States division of the adoption agency were asked to testify against him, attesting to the amount of money they had sent over for the children that he used. He was sent to prison. The problem was that the other people that were running the Korean part of the agency were his relatives. They were "punishing" the United States division of the adoption agency by not releasing the children to their families. You were one of the children stuck in the middle of that! On the other side, we were one of the families in agony waiting for our child to come home.

Finally, the day came when they called from the adoption agency. They told us to have the documents ready in one day, as there seemed to be a window of time that they were going to release the children who were already assigned to families. They did not know how long the Korean government would honor this agreement, so they were making a special trip to Korea to present the documents and hopefully bring the children back. I think you were the oldest of 10-children that the Korean government was going to release. A week later the adoption agency called and said to come to the airport, your son would be here tomorrow. That evening they called again and said, don't come to the airport. My heart sank again. I was relieved to find out that all the children had just gotten sick on the airplane; they were going to make a stop over in Japan.

Finally, the call came about 4 or 5 days later, to come to the Seattle airport the next evening to pick you up! That day could not go fast enough, we were finally on our way to the airport. As we drove the two-hour trip, my stomach got sicker and sicker. When we got to the airport, I ran straight into the bathroom and threw up! I was nauseated and thought I had the flu. While we were waiting at the arrival gate we met most of the other families. Most of them were from Oregon and Montana. They had all driven great lengths and were just as anxious as we were from all the delays and waiting.

Finally, the plane arrived. I was not sure if I could even stand up. I felt so sick. The flight attendants had everyone else depart the plane first. It was pure agony for most of us parents to have to stand behind a barrier, straining our necks, to catch a glimpse of our child walking down the airplane ramp. Finally, we saw the adoption agency escorts carrying out the children. One mother broke through the barrier, grabbed her baby out of the escort's arms and took off running down the hallway, crying and hugging her baby, holding her tightly against her chest. She ran until the hallway ended, and then sat down on the floor crying and rocking her baby. Her husband and two other children were running behind her. They collapsed to the floor. All of them were crying and hugging the baby.

They kept bringing out babies. I wondered if I would recognize you from the pictures like the other mothers did. You were the last one out of the plane! I recognized you in the arms of the escort immediately! She handed you over to me and we sat down and talked for a few minutes. You looked so tired and bewildered. She told us that you were so cute on the plane. You would eat anything in sight and when you had finished your food, you would go and stand by other passengers, just staring at their plates of food, so people on the plane started giving you their food. She said your little belly was bulging it was so full.

Your adoption papers said you were almost five years old, but you were so small! We didn't think the age was appropriate. I was holding you, and smiling at you, trying to talk with a tone of voice to make you feel safe. You could not understand English and I had no idea how much you were told or understood what was happening. As we were walking out of the airport, I realized I was not sick anymore. In fact, it had completely left the moment they handed you to us. I realized it was anxiety, not the flu. I've never had that feeling happen before or since. There was so much peace in my heart once you were finally in my arms. It had been almost nine months to the day that I first contacted the agency about adopting you!!

It was late driving back from the airport. I held you all the way home (that was before car seat days). We stopped in Tacoma, Washington and bought you a roast beef sandwich. I held you in the car and showed you how to eat it. You did not like the bread or cheese, but you ate the meat out of it. I bought a little stuffed dog for you and brought it in the car. You wrapped your little arms around that dog the whole way home. I remember holding you in the car and thinking how much I loved you. It was no different than when they laid my newborn baby girls in my arms. You were loved just as much as they were, if not more. There was even a deeper feeling that I'd never experienced with the girls. I think back and wonder if it was a sense of protectiveness because of what you had already gone through. I loved you immediately. As I got to know you I was "in love" with you, the same as I got to know my little girls personalities.

We arrived home at about 2AM from the airport. I think your aunt Suzanne was watching the girls. We woke the girls up to come and meet you. I sat you down on the floor in the front room. Shanie was five, Dana was three and a half, and Sherri was two and a half years old. All three of your sisters came up. They had an instant bonding with you. They knew their brother was coming home soon and had been waiting the whole nine-month process. After a minute Sherri, turned around and went back down stairs to her bedroom. She brought up three special toys that she would not let Shanie or Dana even touch, and laid them in your lap!! I was shocked, it brought tears to my eyes, as it was her way of saying you are my brother, and even Suzanne said it was amazing! Sherri would scream if Shanie or Dana even looked as if they were going to touch those three little toys (one was a stuffed pink cat, a blue beanbag doll, and a rubber cupid doll. She'd carry those three toys in her arms all day long and play with them as she waited for you to arrive. From that time on, she would let only you play with them.

I put you in a sleeping bag on the floor that night next to our bed. The adoption agency said you had not slept in a bed before, so I did not want to put you downstairs, for your first night, in a foreign bed in your new room. That morning you were so sick with fever and diarrhea. I put you in the bathtub at about 6AM. While you were in the tub, Grandpa Schmidt came over (he never came that early) and had a 4-foot red fire engine in his arms for you. He asked if you were awake. I told him you were sick and in the tub. He tip toed to the bathroom and peaked in. His first words were with a big smile, "Sho-o-o-o-o-o-o-t HE SURE IS CUTE!!!!

The first two weeks went fairly smooth; you were so cute and everything was new and exciting for you. Your favorite toys were an empty macaroni and cheese box and a gold butter box. You found them in the garbage can. You would hold them and smell them. You'd go to sleep with them. I'd take them out of your bed when you were asleep and put them back in the garbage can. In the morning when you woke up, you'd come straight to the garbage can take them out and hold them

13

and smell them all day again. I did that for about four days! Finally, I stopped taking them out of your bed at night; I thought I might be training you to think the garbage can was a toy box!

    After two weeks you seemed to get really angry and frustrated. I thought it was because you could not communicate. You never even tried to speak to us in Korean; I think you knew we would not be able to understand you. One exception was one day when I was emptying the dishwasher. You came over and started handing me dishes to put in the cupboard. You grabbed a pewter cup that was still hot from the drying cycle and started screaming something in Korean at me. You didn't want to drop the cup, but it was burning your little fingers. So I started trying to teach you words. You already knew "Gum". Uncle Dick taught you that your second day. So, when you would come to the sink and whine for a drink, I would say "water", "water" about four or five times, and then you would repeat it and I'd give you a drink of water. I did the same with "potty", only I didn't press it too much! You were quick and within a week you had already learned so many words.

I love you to pieces!!!

Love, Mom

II

My Adopted Family

It's not real life for a child to learn that they have no factual beginning to their so-called life. Rather, it was re-constructed through adoption records, court documents, a series of bone age tests and a walk through memory lane from the ones close enough to remember, in their own words, how the beginning of your life came to be. For me, that was real life, not make believe. The memory lane constructing my life that said I was found on the steps of a police station in Seoul, Korea. My mind wonders what that must have felt like. Did I cry? Did I scream? Did I keep getting up and chase after my family as they left me there? Did they have to push me down on the stairs and run away before I could regain balance on my two feet? Or did I just wait for my mom to return? Did I just wait staring at the ground? Did I peek up to see if they were getting closer? Were they? Where did they go? Maybe they were hiding behind a corner until the hands of a policeman grabbed me from the cold stairs, holding me until the doors of the police station shut behind us as we entered into my new reality. These memories and feelings I no longer have.

Nonetheless I was placed in a Catholic orphanage in Seoul, Korea called White Lilly. The orphanage reports say I was compliant, neat and withdrawn. After six to nine months I was adopted by Brad and Nancy Owen who had three daughters, Shanie, Dana and Sherri. They lived in Shelton Washington.

My new father, Brad, was a small business owner and aspiring politician. Today he is the Lieutenant Governor for the State of Washington. He resides as President of the Senate and is also the founder and president of a substance abuse and anti-bullying effort he developed in the late 1980's. His accomplishments have been acknowledged with a PHD in Humanities. He currently lives in Shelton, Washington with his new wife, Linda.

My new mom, Nancy, was a homemaker and activist in the church. Today she is the founder and president of an adoption agency that operates offices located throughout the world. They assist with the development of adoption laws within third world countries and process adoptions all over the world. She currently lives in Yuma, Arizona with her new husband Terry.

My oldest sister Shanie, currently lives in Budapest with her husband Peter, and three daughters Elizabeth, Amanda and Cammi-Ann. They are missionaries in Eastern Europe who empower young people all over the world to change people's lives through the healing power of the word of God.

My middle sister Dana currently lives in Yuma, Arizona with her husband Dennis and five kids Casey, Savannah, Joshua, Seth and Sophia. Dana is a homemaker. They are actively involved with their church and youth functions. Dennis works in the plumbing/construction industry.

My little sister Sherri currently lives in Yuma, Arizona with her husband Matt and their two daughters Naomi and Jaidyn. Sherri is a homemaker and graduate of Western Washington University, while Matt is employed as an occupational therapist.

My little brother Adam, who will be later adopted into our family as narrated in the following chapters of my parents divorce, currently lives in Olympia, Washington with his new bride Miranda. He is an Assistant Manager for a prominent telecom company, while Miranda is certified dental assistant. She is also working towards her masters in Archaeology. She would eventually like to obtain her PHD in Egyptology.

My youngest brother Royce, will also be introduced to our family as narrated in the later chapters of my dad's second marriage. He currently lives in Wyoming with his wife Carrie and son Luke. He is a freelance artist and Carrie is a Captain for the Air force.

My new family lived in a yellowish two-story home on Ellinor Street in Shelton, Washington. It had a long pebbled driveway that sat parallel to the front of the house. There were four distinctly different sections of the yard that were completely fenced in, with two sides surrounded by trees and an alley. The front yard was raised with a walkway down the middle, the main yard, to the left side of the house, was huge and sloped downward, providing an endless field of lawn to play in. The backyard had a patio with a basketball hoop and a small grassy area filled with cherry trees. The right side of the house was covered with trees and bushes. It always had dark, lingering shadows, making it kind of scary to walk through. I don't ever actually remember walking all the way from one end to the other end of the house down the scary side of the yard.

On the main floor of the inside of the house there was the master bedroom, a second bedroom that had a huge elevated closet that always made me feel creepy inside, a bathroom, living room, kitchen and laundry room. The stairs in the kitchen led to the downstairs, where there was another bedroom, a large playroom that had two beds for Dana and Sherri, and a side room that connected the two, but we never really walked through. The lights were always burnt out and it also had a creepy feel to it. This is the house I would start my new life in.

Now I have a new mom, new dad, three new sisters and a new house to live in. However, I still don't have an agreed upon birth date. Apparently children born in many Asian countries are born as a one-year-old child. My parents did not agree with my inherited age. They took me to a pediatrician who was experienced with Asian orphans. The pediatrician performed a bone age test, psychological exams and a test of physical skills to determine my age. He felt I was about three and a half years old, as did my mother. The pediatrician wrote a letter attesting their findings, which were presented by my parent's attorney to the court at the time of my adoption. They requested that my date of birth be changed to better reflect my probable age. This was a turning point in my life. I was no longer Lee Yong Yul with an arbitrary birth date of March 5th 1971. I was now Mark Lee Owen with a September 5, 1972 date of birth, 25 days older than my middle sister Dana, and about a year or so in-between my little sister Sherri and oldest sister Shanie. I was officially three and a half years old.

I now have an American birth certificate with a new birth date, social security number, name and family. I was armed and ready to face the challenges of the world with my new identity. It wasn't me though. In fact, the transformation really created a new me that would later be confused with the old me, leaving the actual me somewhere lost in the middle constantly trying to adapt or adopt new surroundings.

Although I should have felt an overwhelming sense of peace and gratitude for being rescued from a world that abandoned me, instead, I felt lonely, lost and confused. My adoption was a continual reminder to me that I did not belong. I would sit in my room for hours dreaming of just fitting in and being normal. What is normal? Is it the color of your skin? The shape of your eyes? The bridge of your nose? The sounds accenting the language in which you speak?

I took on American characteristics trying to develop friendships throughout life with mostly Americans. Why? Because the warped reality that I lived under the assumption that the entire Korean culture abandoned me because I was not good enough. Rather than being rejected again, I worked hard to distance myself from other Asians throughout most of my life, so that I could be part of my new culture and claim ownership in my new family.

The comfort I had by living the façade that I was exactly the same as my new family would work until I looked in a mirror, or saw a picture of myself. I hated pictures of me. I don't want to be different! But I am different. For starters, I'm Asian, not white, and that was only the outside. I tried to fit in. I tried to please. I tried to always be a good child, always wanting to please others so that I would never be asked to leave again. However, it didn't matter whether I was in a crowded room hidden behind my forced laughter, or completely isolated laying awake in my bed at night, in my loneliest of hours, "don't reject me", was the crying plea I would only voice to myself.

I remember a time visiting some friends of my parents. They were business partners of them. They had a two-story home in Shelton, Washington, where they lived with their three kids. One evening as we were all playing downstairs, the kids began picking on me, poking fun and telling me that whales ate my real parents! Ha, ha. Na-na-na-na-boo-boo! Just childish fun. What it felt like was a bunch of kids holding hands hopping, skipping and laughing while they circled me getting closer and closer and the words got slower and slower as I sat in a fetal position on the ground until I couldn't breathe anymore as I began to hyperventilate. But what really happened was that I ran out of the house covering my ears. I looked back and they were all pointing and laughing at me through the sliding glass door. I stopped, turned around, "CLICK", the door locked. I'm alone. It's dark. I feel moisture in the air. I hear crickets and a howling sound from the cold wind. Let me in. I stare at the glass door and voice these words ever so softly to myself. Let me in. I won't run anymore. I won't be scared anymore. I won't make you stop saying things to me anymore. Let me in... Please.

That was one of the scariest moments I ever remember feeling. I stood in fear begging them to let me back in. I didn't cry though, I was too scared for my life. No protectors from the vicious world that has already rejected and abandoned me. I wanted to be in the protection of people. I felt I would die otherwise. Looking in the glass doors everything was slow motion. The kids were jumping around, laughing and pointing at me. Just let me in...please. I was so scared inside. This was my physical reminder as I looked on my reflection from the glass door of being on the outside and never belonging to anybody or anywhere. Not even to myself, just a reflection of something that resembles me. It wasn't me though. It couldn't be. My existence would not be based on my inferiorities. I couldn't allow it. That fear is what I used to fuel my fantasy of who I could be. I created a person to destroy the one in the reflection of the glass door. A person that was popular, smart, attractive, loved, accepted and the envy of everyone. His name was Mike. I wanted to be him.

So that was my beginning. Factual or not, it's who I was told that I was. A life that would be changed by the courts to disassociate myself from the biological roots that said I was not fit to live in the world that I was born into. A factual beginning changed into an imaginary one to be raised in a culture that wasn't mine by a family that I did not genealogically belong to.

It doesn't surprise me to reflect how sad and alone I always felt. It doesn't surprise me that I felt so worthless yet to afraid to cry for help in fear that these tears would expose imperfections within myself that would become a burden onto my new family and force them to remove me from their life, just like I was already accustomed too and un-like the closeness a child has with its mother, I was born, abandoned, and created a make believe beginning that led to a dysfunctional foundation that I would house years of internal suffering while the rest of the world, with good reason, peered in with disapproving eyes for the self-destructing behaviors I would later do in attempt to self medicate the trauma suffered as an abandoned child. It doesn't surprise me that because of the pain of abandonment I could only interpret reality through a filter of rejection and distrust.

III

Borrowed Family / Borrowed Culture / Borrowed Time

One of my earliest memories that I have was with my mom and my little sister Sherri. We were all sitting in the kitchen on Christmas Eve talking about Christmas, Santa Clause, reindeer, cookies and, uh huh, presents! Lots of presents. My grandparents had just left and my mom was folding clothes trying to persuade us to go to bed. During my mom's lecture that Santa Clause would not bring presents until we went to bed, I looked outside the big rectangular kitchen window and saw a silhouette of Santa Clause and his reindeers flying in front of the moon. My face lit up so huge. I grabbed my folded clothes off the table and ran down stairs to go to bed. The anticipation was killing me. I kept peaking out the windows and listening for Santa Clause on the roof. I fell asleep before I could actually give Santa Clause his milk and cookies, but when I awoke the next morning…wow, I've never seen such a bright Christmas tree and so many presents! I remember the bright red wagon I got. It was so huge it couldn't be wrapped. Just a big red bow and ribbon.

For me, this is how I imagined life was meant to be. Innocent children living innocent lives with their mom and dad and siblings, playing in innocent fairly tale worlds that once a year included Santa Clause himself. But I could never feel the overwhelming feelings of joy for very long. Happiness always conflicted with sadness. I was never sure which feelings I were supposed to have, which ones I wasn't, and how to process either. Ultimately all feelings were eventually pushed down and ignored causing a detachment from reality itself. This made me feel like I was just a spectator in a borrowed family, without a real birthday, and causing great internal anguish that needed a way out. But was there ever relief in site?

Another happy childhood memory I have is playing for hours in our playroom downstairs in the Ellinor Street house. I had a very vivid imagination and could get lost for what seemed like days playing army, drums and even house with my sisters. It was my world, my make believe world. As I got older my parents did some remodeling and we had a new dining room upstairs, and an office area added downstairs that was eventually turned into a bedroom. The addition downstairs was real creepy to me. It was at the bottom of a long stairwell that was always dark. There was a sliding glass door in the back of the bedroom that led to the patio in the backyard. I remember at night being scared to go downstairs. I was always in fear of seeing something outside those doors.

During this time of my life I had a best friend named Kari. Kari lived in a home about two blocks up the street from ours. Her home is what I thought was a large trailer or manufactured type home. Kari had chin length blonde hair, freckles and was just a guy's type of guy. We did everything together. We played army man in the huge yard, walked around the block, played house, laughed and giggled like adolescents do. My largest disappointment came when I asked if Kari could stay over-night so we could have a slumber party. My parents sat me down on the couch and had a serious conversation with me. Mark, Kari is not a boy. What? Yes, Kari is a girl! I was embarrassed and felt humiliated. How could this be? I wanted to be my father's son. A boy. No, a man that liked cars, rockets, hunting and worms. Now my best friend is a girl? I was mortified inside. I did not want to give them, my new parents, any reason to send me back to Korea with a defective stamp and a request a new child. Say, a real boy this time? I felt I had to reject Kari to ensure my fear of being rejected would not become a reality. I had to protect my new domain. Consequently I don't have a lot of memories of Kari after this time.

My new best friend was Simon. He was a bleached blonde boy this time and I was a black haired Korean. My mom would call us salt and pepper. You couldn't separate us. Weekend slumber parties, playing board games all night, and guarding the bedroom door as we snuck into his parent's room to look at the nude magazines under the bed. Simon was fun, but really just another stage in the development of life for me. Although we remained friends for years to come, he was really just another milestone in my quest to adapt to my new surroundings. A painful memory for me to realize how I perceived even his friendship, like my entire life, as only temporary and some type of lesson or experience to learn from. Never able to just accept the fact that it is simply what it is, a friendship.

Then I met Joey. His family lived a couple blocks from us. Their house was really small. He shared a room with his older brother that always talked about leaving for the army one day. I never realized at the time, but Joey's family was really poor. I just thought they were messy.

The combination of my two friends allowed me a place in this world for a while. Simon was gigglier, ha, ha, let's sneak around the house or stay up all night playing board games. A who cares about tomorrow type of guy. Joey was more focused and seemed to have things in life he was always thinking about. Seemed to have a detachment issue with his older brother. His family was dysfunctional. I don't ever remember meeting his dad. Joey was real guarded. Kept people at bay. I think I was a combination of the two of them. That's what sparked my interest. Although I was un-sure of myself, one thing I knew is that my personality could be easily changed based on the people I associated with. This character trait became more and more evolved, as I got older. Constantly absorbing and living as somebody else and never really knowing who I was. Never claiming ownership or becoming too attached to any of my decisions or actions. Deep inside nothing was ever me, just a role I would play in different environments.

My detachment issues and ability to absorb personalities rather than develop my own made it easy for me to feel at home as a character in the Town parade my mom would put us in. One year I was the tin man from the wizard of oz, and another year I was Oscar the grouch. As kids, we would become very excited to pick out our costumes to wear during the parade. We would walk up and down the city streets as people would clap and cheer and we would throw them candy. It was one of the Town's biggest events. However, I always had a sense of fun and a sense of overwhelming anxiety or fear at the same time. At one point I would be brave and lost in part of the excitement. The other feeling I was a scarred little boy clinging onto his mother's hand. These overwhelming feelings would force me to wear a smile on the outside to hide myself on the inside. I would force my mouth to make an upward arch, resembling a smile, and my eyes would squint a little bit. Inside I could never experience the freeing feeling that a smile produces. Even when I dreamed I wore the same internal face. I can't pinpoint the exact time in life that I forgot how to smile. Or, for that matter, the exact time in life that I ever learned how to smile.

Nonetheless there were so many people at the parades that my mind had to shut them out. Laughing and cheering people made me feel sad. They made me feel like the kid that didn't belong. Especially now that I was being paraded through the City streets. I guess how I really felt was "meet the adopted kid, he has no real family or birthday. All you kids with a real mom and dad, wad up a fistful of candy and get ready to throw it at the adopted kid." Yeah, let's put him in a goofy costume too. Although it was one of my favorite characters from Sesame Street, being Oscar the Grouch hurt me. It was a green suit that covered my face while I wore a garbage can around my waist. On the inside that's how I really felt. Someone whose face should be hidden from society and left in a garbage can.

As life in the Ellinor house began it's final phase, around the age of six my father sponsored HB 4 that was signed into law in the late 70's by Washington State's then Governor Dixie Lee Ray. It's intent was to remove unnecessary government bureaucracy and allow all foreign born kids adopted to Washington residents to receive Washington State birth certificates making it easier to obtain things like a drivers license, checking account, car loan and even admission into higher education. My mother saved the picture of the Governor and the pen that was used to sign the bill into law. The rewarding effects of the law becomes more apparent as I get older and see a generation of foreign-born adoptees receiving Washington State birth certificates without the knowledge of the ones before them that struggled to find identity without identification.

My lonely days at the Ellinor house would not last forever though. When I was about seven or eight my parents sold that house and moved into a huge four-story house on West Harvard Street. It was on top of a huge hill that over-looked the forest. It was the only house on that side of the street. Everyone thought it was a mansion. We called it the White House. It was set in a huge yard and surrounded by wooded areas that we could build forts and play for hours. The entire neighbor kids came to our house for youth groups, church functions and just to play. We had a basketball hoop and a shed that we had a rooster, chickens and two little pygmy goats. We had rope swings and endless outdoor adventures in the woods.

The main floor of the house had a bathroom off to the right, a kitchen to the left, and a huge staircase at the end of the hall leading upstairs. We had a large dining room and living room that covered half the main floor and a TV room off to the side and a balcony across the entire front room. The downstairs was a huge garage and un-finished basement and the 3rd floor had a large corner bathroom and 5-bedrooms; 4 out of 5 had balconies overlooking the woods. I was always jealous because my oldest sister had her own private balcony. As kids we would always debate who would take her room after she moved out and married.

My sisters Dana, Sherri and I would go out in the woods at the Harvard house and play boxcar children. We discovered so many things out there. There was one special broken tree we would climb over. We would balance one by one walking foot in front of foot in fear of falling off. Why, the crocodiles of course! If we fell off the log we would land in crocodile infested water. In the spring there would be wild Daffodils in that infested water. It's because of these times; Daffodils are one of Dana's favorite flowers. There is also the time we discovered all the apple trees in our woods. We would spend so many afternoons building forts and trying to figure out how to pick the apples and bring them home. There were also a section of woods that we found a little shack.

We were all convinced it was a home for witches. None of us could get the courage to ever get close enough to find out.

My oldest sister Shanie discovered a whole in the attic wall that we could hide in. We used to play in it, and act like we were hiding out as if a war had broke out. That was our hiding place. Like the Jews in World War ll. Then of course I can't stop from sleepwalking. There were nights that I would sleep walk and Shanie would see my reflection in the mirrors along the stairs and start screaming as if there was a predator in our home. My mother would quietly sneak down the stairs to see who it was (how terrifying for her), and there I would be sound asleep on the couch. In the mean time my three sisters would be huddled in mom's bed frightened.

Although we had many activities and childhood fun, the distortion from my blinders stemming from my abandonment made me feel incomplete and on an endless search for something more. I never knew what it was though. Play, laugh, smile, and then nothing. Lights off. No feelings anymore. Nothing more to absorb, distract or become. It was in the four walls of my room in this house that I remember dreaming the most. I was tucked away in this huge house peeking out the window seal. I would dream of having friends. Lots and lots of friends. I would be popular and everyone would like me. They would love me and want me to stay forever. They would never let me feel this feeling of being alone again. So alone, that as each day passed by, it it was becoming more and more difficult for me to process and accept the love from the family I had in front of me from my three sisters, mother and father. Surrounded by happiness but all alone inside. To afraid to accept in fear I would be rejected. I wanted to take the chance though. I couldn't.

So as memories fade back and forth, the solid memories I have of my mother, at an early age, was her getting us ready in the morning before school. My only real memory of my dad was when he promised to teach me how to throw a football. He was walking from the bathroom towards their bedroom. Otherwise, as far as I can remember, my parents were very busy. So, like society does, after school we would come home to meet our baby-sitter. She would help us do homework and feed us dinner. We would often have different characters to play during dinner. We would stand on our chair and say how our day at school went in the voice of our character. My funniest memory was all of us huddled under the dining room table one night during a thunder and lightning storm.

So we had a big house, huge yards and forests, built in playmates with my three sisters, a babysitter and lots of toys. However, there was something very apparent that was missing in this equation. Think. Think. What more could a kid want? What were those things again? Ummmm, we had a big house, huge yards and forests, built in playmates...yeah, yeah, yeah. What is missing here? Maybe I could ask my sisters if they felt like something was missing? Maybe I could ask my babysitter if something was missing? I know the response though. Sorry, wait until your parents get home. Good one. Wait until my parents get home. Thanks. Now I know what's missing. Where are my parents? Of course this is the internal question I would in reality only ask myself. Where are they? My adopted parents? My biological parents? How come I don't know this? This and so much more.

Growing up I longed to have my parents around. I wanted them there for dinner, movies, even when we played our Sound of Music Characters. Their absence was a painful reminder of the biological parents that had already been removed from my life. For an abandoned child this is a terminal combination. A double negative that does not make a positive. No amount of love or anything new could ever replace what was already lost in my heart until I was able to process the feelings associated with my abandonment. Suppress the feelings. Avoid the pain. Push down. Gone. But for how long? All feelings must resurface and if not prepared, well, you'll see.

One night I decided to run away. I walked out the front door, no jacket, no over night bag of clothes, no toothbrush, no money, no food. My oldest sister chased me up the street. I didn't cry. I didn't feel. I listened to her say mom's going to be so mad when she comes home. I processed that for a moment and came back home. I guess that's what I needed to hear at the time to feel wanted. But when was mom going to be home? When was dad going to be home? All I remember is a huge empty house that had the entire family in it maybe once or twice a year. Not even birthdays could get my mom and dad in the same room at the same time. If judging by my memory sake, I would have only had two birthdays up until this point. One at a fast food restaurant and one I only re-live through photographs. I know there is more though. Well, not with both parents together.

Christmas seems to be one of the only times that I can really remember having both parents together. And there was only a small handful at that. I remember one year I came home from school and the TV room was off limits. I crept downstairs and peaked in one night. There were endless bags taller than me of toys and gifts. Great big brown bags overflowing with stuff. Wow. That was one of the few Christmas's I remember the entire family together. I will always cherish that time. Not because of all the material gifts but because the memory I have of all of us together as a family, my emotional gifts. Months later my mom found hidden behind her dresser a pin-up solar system that she had forgotten she had bought for me. That was like getting a Christmas gift in February. It glowed in the dark so I would purposely leave the light on during the day so at night I could fall asleep to the stars and planets. Maybe the stars up in space freely floating safely away from anything painful on earth is where I truly felt was the safest place for me to be.

However, as wounded and alone as I felt growing up I could not deny the soft heart that I had. During slug months I couldn't watch, as my mom would throw salt on them. Inside I could feel their pain, like their bodies were crinkling up and they would scream in horror as they held on to tiny bits of life before it was all over for them. My sisters and I banded together to stop the senseless killings. Can you imagine little children with picket signs? Okay, probably a mere fabrication of the actual events that occurred. Perhaps a bit dramatic. Dana reminds me of the reality of my actions, as I would fling the slugs with a shovel on the roof of the house, or squash them in the lawn with the bottom of my shoes. Gross! Some things cause reactions that we often take from one extreme to the other. Dr. Jekyl, meet Mr. Hyde. Love life, destroy life.

We decide to save all the dying animals in our yard. We would save birds and shrews that our cat would attack and try to nurse them back to health. Sherri would stand guard keeping the cat away and I would use leaves and paper to pick up the half dead animals. The shrew was the funniest. We put him in a little cage on the balcony off my room. Gave it food and water. We made a little chair out of cardboard and would sit him in it like we were having a tea party. We came home from school one day and it was dead. My sisters and I had a funeral and buried it in the back yard. So that was that. My sister Sherri talked about wanting to be a veterinarian and I moved on to my next exploration of personality.

The next one was curious. Although I was extremely compliant I very subtly tested my boundaries by pushing the edge just a little bit. One time I shot my sister Dana in the head with a BB gun. Ummm, maybe a little to far with this one. The gun itself you had to pump full of air and even then it would barely shoot a BB. Nonetheless I pulled the trigger when she walked off the downstairs porch. She screamed, grabbed the top of her head and fell to the ground. I threw down the BB gun. I wanted to jump over the balcony and make sure she was alive. I didn't. I ran across my room, through the hall, down the stairs, passing the living room, and out the back door, over the porch and down the final stairs only to see her laughing hysterically at me. As old as the gun was I'd be lucky if the BB even left the barrel let alone actually hit her. To this day I still can't stand the sight of guns. Ironically, my adopted brother Adam, I know, not in our family yet, keep reading, attempted the same trick later in his life when he was twelve with a neighbor girl. He wanted to prove that the BB gun was not loaded. He pumped the gun, aimed and squeezed the trigger. Oops, he shot himself in the pointer finger on his left hand. Apparently there was one remaining BB stuck in the chamber. He was rushed to a doctor that pulled out the BB. Imagine if he had actually shot the girl in the head?

So that was a defining moment in life for me. It reaffirmed to me that life events and their boundaries and limits were, well, only imaginary. The gun and BB did not really exist, just like the pain I was harboring inside as long as I pretended it did not exist. I could change the course of anything by simply erasing what I didn't want to be true. This may come in handy as I attempt to hurdle larger and larger internal struggles. My new life struggle was to erase myself again and find a new identity. This identity had to have a built in mechanism to protect me from the evils of this world. The evils of this world in my head that told me people are going to, and will always, reject me. The people in my world that were currently rejecting me were my adopted parents.

The people that had already rejected me were my biological family. They had no time for me. At least not the amount of time that I felt I needed as an abandoned child attempting to leave those feelings behind to embrace the love provided by his new family. The love that was to replace the loneliness inside. I was convinced I could fabricate this type of love though. Maybe not from my parent's involvement, but by having a lot of friends. Not just make believe friends anymore but a lot of actual real live people.

At such a small age I had already fully embraced my new journey. I watched what popular kids did and mimicked their actions. I sat at the cool table doing mean boy pranks while hurting the hearts of the girls at school. Is that not what an adolescent boy should do? I was just a child. Unfortunately so were they. Just kids longing for affection. I had a lot of people wanting to be my friend but I got to reject them to maintain coolness. No one could be around me until I chose. I was becoming the popular kid at school. I no longer had to live the abandoned victim. Or was I perpetuating these feelings that much more. A world of people I would never know, making it harder and harder to express my insecurities and fears because it appeared that I must have everything together.

I thought that having friends and being popular would take away my feelings of being alone and remove my pain of being abandoned. From the first grade forward was my earliest memory of trying to maintain status with the popular crowd. People would follow what I did. I knew it was all make believe though. My quest for friends was actually backfiring. Although it appeared I was attracting a lot of friendships, inside I knew I was really attracting a lot of followers that I could make do anything I wanted. I remember in the fourth grade sticking up for the loser in our school that was going to get beat up. I didn't fight; I just made sure he didn't get hit. The principal thought I was in the fight, they never new it was the other kid. Unfortunately I didn't do it for the protection of him, I did it to prove in my mind that people are so shallow that the voice of a popular kid could change the assumptions of others. That is the sad reality that I lived in. Draw people in just to prove they aren't sincere so I can push them away and remain guarded and closed. Really wanting affection yet hating people inside. They were all passing my tests that would prove them shallow in one way or another. The ultimate test that in the end I was the only

one that ever really lost. Robbed of the beauty of ever having inter-
personal relationships with anybody.

      I also learned at a pretty early age that I was very intelligent
for my grade level. After the first grade the school wanted me to skip
the second grade. My mother wanted me to stay with my classmates.
By the time I got to the third grade I was completing assignments so
quickly that my teacher thought I was disrupting the class and
somehow cheating. Educationally I didn't invest much time into
textbooks after that. It was too easy. I would just do the homework,
study before a test to ace it. Although I respected him, I remember
thinking to myself how could a teacher be this ignorant?

      I don't quite remember the exact chain of events, but one day
the entire family loaded into the car and we were on our way to pick up
our new brother. Like me, he was abandoned as a toddler in Korea,
placed in an orphanage and later adopted by an American family. We
drove from Shelton to Olympia, which was about 30-minutes. I
remember the house had a small cement front porch with a large,
wooden door. Ding-dong. That's the doorbell. The woman that
answered had this little boy off to her left side halfway hidden behind
her. His name is Adam. Adam was originally brought to the United
States to be adopted. His adoptive family gave him up after one year.
He was placed in a foster home for three weeks. Although the foster
home was very nice, it was clear by the scars on Adam's arm that there
was probably mental abuse in the adoptive home, and "possibly"
physical abuse as well. We don't know, it's just the fingernail scars
were not on the records from Korea that my mother originally received.
They were well-healed scars by the time he was placed in the foster
home that we picked him up from. What traumatic events, disguised as
love, did he suffer from the families that had "rescued" him? At age
five he had already lived a lifetime of emotional hurt. To this day at the
age of 28, he only remembers one foster family, but he was actually
with at least two or three families. He has blocked out in his
subconscious memory the dark past that lies hidden in his head.

      He has such a big heart. I remember when we were leaving
and the entire neighborhood of kids were saying goodbye. Adam
thought a collection of cars were his and wanted to take them with him.
His foster siblings really wanted to keep them. He asked me what he

should do. I was already a big brother. I told him to leave them with him because his new house had a playroom full of toys that spanned the entire fourth floor of his new house. You should have seen the look on his face when we got him home. He fell asleep up there playing in his new playroom. He would always ask my mom how long we were going to keep him. She would say forever. The sad part that I know like me he won't have the same memories of these events that I do. The pain that lies within the heart of an abandoned child steals away any memory that may have been created too close to a bad one. Memories are collected in blocks of time and locked away under the painful vault that life has created that may never be opened again. For this reason I will know when I look in his eyes that those happy feelings exist within him, just like I'm sure they do within my own heart of pains.

IV

Divorce #%!*

The effects from my childhood trauma were magnified when my mother informed us that our father was moving out and they were headed for divorce. I think I was already being prepared for this before we had any real conversations about it. It's not as if he was ever there in the first place. The church pastor and my mom sat us all on the couch in the living room. She began to talk and stopped. She had tears running down her face. Everything in my tiny world began to get really big. Overwhelmingly large, unmanageable feelings. Control. I was losing. I felt like a small person sitting with their hands in their lap on an oversized chair that there was no way down from. Voices faded. I don't remember all the words that were said.

Huh? How does an already abandoned child supposed to process the feelings associated with another family collapse? How is this child supposed to accept that the family that rescued him no longer wants to remain together? How is this child not supposed to feel the rejection that reinforces the trauma from his childhood abandonment that this new family was supposed to have rescued him from ever feeling again? Even though I do not remember every word that was said I do know how the feelings were being unfolded in my heart. I cry sometimes today as these feelings reappear and I try and make them go away. Tough. That's what I am forced to be.

During my parents separation my father moved temporarily into a trailer and then back to the smaller home on Ellinor Street. Eventually we were introduced to Linda and Royce that would later become his wife and son, his new family, my replacement. I remember one weekend visit finding a toy in my dad's car, it was yellow, I think it was a duck. That was before we were officially informed of other people in his life, but that's when I knew. The feeling of hope that I would cling onto that the separation was all temporary, was slowing being destroyed. I was sad but I didn't know how to feel. I didn't feel. I just pretended it wasn't real, you weren't real, this car wasn't real, this life wasn't real, and neither was this yellow duck. It wasn't real. Go away!

It was around this time that I met a new best friend. His name was Mark. He had a mom, a dad and a sister. His family became my surrogate family. They would take me on camping trips, church outings and Mark and I would have slumber parties talking about owning business's that we'd call "M and M Fix It" and repair BMX bikes. We'd stay up till wee hours in the morning talking about the neighbor girls and sneaking out to meet them late at night.

One camping trip over 4th of July weekend Mark and I snuck off to listen to AC DC. The song, we've got big balls. I was scared to listen in fear of getting caught. I knew it was the devils' music. After all, the name stood for After Christ Devil Comes. All the school kids that listened to that kind of music had ratty long hair, ripped jeans, earrings and looked gross. I was a preppy kid. Collared shirts, pressed jeans and combed hair. Hmmm. I was headed for trouble. Late that night we came back from playing on the beach at the ocean with a collection of fireworks we found. We threw them in the campfire. Holy smokes. Stuff started shooting every direction. We were locked in the back of the camper truck the rest of the night. The next day Mark, his dad and I packed our bikes and headed for the trails. The bikes were so heavy. His dad said no but we insisted we take them. He wouldn't help us get them up the trails, over the logs, through the creeks. We were wiped out. At one point I told him we should just leave the bikes behind and get new ones. His dad said no to that.

We finally made it to the rope swing. Hurrah! We would jump off the bank; grab the rope and swing back and forth, free as bird with nothing from this world holding us down. Mark slipped and landed on the ground. His head landed gently placed between two sharp rocks. Not even enough room between the two for him to move but up and off the ground. God saved his life and rope swinging was now done. I have yet in life to swing on another one. At the time, I was not sure of the lessons I would learn from Mark and his family. I do know it was a friendship and surrogate family that made me feel part of something. Perhaps a family that did family functions together. Both mom and dad at the same time. Perhaps it was having a perfect friend. Perhaps in my mind he was a real live Mike, my made up twin brother. Or maybe just another façade of what I was feeling I would never have in life.

So with dad officially moved and out, the conversation around the house, if any, referenced him as a *monster*, would follow with my mother running to the church for emotional support. I don't blame her. Where would you go? However, as an over-sensitive abandoned child I felt I was all alone to process these feelings on my own. Go to church; go to the children service during the first break of the morning service. Recite bible versus. Answer questions from the instructor as we learned the parables within the bible. Who was the third apostle? How many did Jesus have? What animal did Joseph and Mary have as they arrived in the stable? How many days did Noah endure the flood? I could get lost. Learning was fun. I even knew most of the answers. Yeah! This is fun. I don't have to think about any of the stuff that is happening at home. Wait. Home. Instant internal frown. Happy. Sad. The pendulum of feelings within my heart had swings that could almost knock me off my feet. I needed to learn to hide what's inside so I wouldn't look that way on the outside. Unstable.

Because of my father's political career, the divorce was all over the newspaper. Kids made fun of us, as kids will do. Nothing really affected me though. Well, at least not on the outside. I was already emotionally secluded. My feelings were already so protected that I didn't let much in, good or bad. I have to believe the feelings were just added to my vault of pains. My sister Dana took the brunt of things. She was harassed by all the kids. I never protected her, I just let them pick. I didn't know what to think. My fantasy of being a part of a real family was being taken away before my very eyes. My life was about to change. It would now include weekend visits to my dad's house, custody battles, bitter arguments of he said she said, and eventually the worst imaginable, my father with a new wife, new son, a new family, I was no longer my father's son, I was being replaced. I'm now replaced...again.

In court I wore a blue suit with really no expression on my face. Just a small child across from divorce attorneys telling the judge whom he wanted to live with. Prior to the hearing our attorney pulled my sister Sherri aside and told her to tell the judge her stomach hurt because she couldn't stand the sight of my dad. I don't remember anything more that happened in court. I've locked it out of my memory. My mind only allows me to remember feelings that create memories of standing outside the courtroom on the cold gray marble floor to scarred to go in the courtroom. Left all alone, abandoned, again. Another reinforcement to the pain I was trying to forget. I didn't' know how to process these feelings. What I really wanted to do is scream and say you said forever! What part of forever did you lie to me about!

I have to entertain that for a moment in time it's not all about me. What about Adam? His new world was compromised the most. He was now going to be thrown into court and the promise for him to stay in our family forever was going to be taken away by the courts. They didn't win though. My mom ended up adopting him as a single parent. Although a positive experience, it unfortunately had un-foreseen adverse affects. While growing up in Hawaii, as I'll later explain, he never really understood what it truly meant to be a child adopted by a single mother. Especially later on in life seeing our mother do home studies for adopting parents, which involve identifying whether or not a family is suitable for taking care of an adoptee. Oddly enough, a single parent is more often than not, deemed un-suitable to adopt a child during a Home Study. What must the chaos be like if leaving a child in this new world is better than the one it would be returned too?

My next real memory was my dad's wedding. It was back at the Ellinor house, my first American home in my memory. I know pronounce you man and wife." I now had a step mom and a stepbrother. Too much to process. I gave her a hug. I didn't even know who she was. Everyone cheered, cried and hugged. In my mind I stepped back into a safe corner. The talking would get louder; the facial expressions would get larger. I would creep further and further back. Oops. I'm stuck. I'm pinned against the corner of the wall in my mind. My own domain, my own world. So, wow, new life? Here I come, I guess.

During the fourth grade we were transferred to another school after my father enrolled Royce in the school we had been attending. Our new school is where I experienced my first form of gambling. I learned to play marbles. The concept is to drop one marble from face level into a slot in a container. If you make it you take one of their marbles. If you miss, you lose yours. I mastered this game. It wasn't long before I had all the cool marbles in school. Then fifth grade started. I had the first video game watch, the first calculator watch, the first cool tape player, the first cool sports bag, etc. I hid behind everything. I disguised myself behind my new friends and now I was hiding myself behind material possessions, which by way of marbles, was turning into greed. I had to have these things to divert the attention of others in fear of the inner me being exposed. The inner child that was lost, confused, alone and afraid. The inner me that was creating more and more barriers to ever being exposed. The inner me that was safely tucked behind his friends and cool gadgets. The inner me that at an early age had to learn how to manipulate his parents to get what he needed to stay hidden from the world.

For the next few years my mom would find her solace by becoming very involved with the church. Her friends would come over at night to watch evening television, we would have youth group functions at our house, and I would try to understand the meaning of life through babysitters, weekend visits with my dad, and adjusting into a new school while trying to make new friends. I shut down quite a bit. I had friends, lots of them, yet I always felt alone. The more friends, the bigger my façade of happiness, the further the pain I pushed down inside. My mom had a support group. Where was mine? Too afraid to cry. To scared to ask for help. Just me suffering, quietly, in silence.

As an adult, Dana reminds me of some of the childhood life we had growing up. Some of the happier times. Like the summer nights we would camp out on our balcony. Or during the winter months when it would snow and we would have all those people from the church over to go sledding down the Harvard Hill. That was so much fun. Mom would have popcorn, and corn/potato chowder, and hot chocolate ready for all the frozen bodies. We would go in to warm up and then right back outside again. It was like a Currier & Ives Christmas card. Then there were the Harvest festival parties we would have in our attic for the youth group. We would make home made doughnuts, and play games like having apples hanging from a string and trying to take a bite out of them with out using our hands, or bobbing for apples. It was harvest time so we had plenty of apples from our apple trees.

Then were the summers with the blackberries that we had tons of. We would pick them for mom and she would make jams and sundae toppings out of them. She's sure there were pies too, but she didn't like blackberries and therefore wouldn't eat them. How about the summer days when mom would take us to Big Rock? We had to hike down that trail. She was always afraid of snakes. We would swim and ride down that little rapid on our inner tubes. Then lay out on the Big Rocks to sunbathe. We always hated the hike back up. These are the childhood memories that she cherishes. I too cherish these memories. They are the ones of the happier times in life.

During this time, my siblings and I spent a lot of time at my aunt and uncle's house, Suzanne and Dave. We would go to the pizza/amusement/what more could a child want pizza parlor with them, listen to music, play games and eat macaroni and cheese and hot dogs. My aunt and uncle became my new surrogate family. Dave would let me sit on his lap in his blue Honda civic and pretend I was driving in the school parking lots. They would take me on fishing trips where I reeled up a boot and a lot of seaweed, never any fish. I asked God to come into my life in their house. I was in the backroom while they prayed over me.

Nonetheless we have to balance the dad factor. Remember? The weekend warrior? Well, as my older sister Shanie informs me that most of our weekend visits with dad were more like bi-monthly, and that it was usually because she called him and asked when we could see him. Although he was allowed to have us every other weekend, he was often busy and rarely took advantage of that time. Shanie would hear my mom crying at night when we lived on Harvard Street. She'd go into her room and try to comfort her. She was in such agony because she didn't know how to pay the bills, feed us kids, or buy us clothes because my dad was not paying child support. She remembers after the divorce, my mom sold her equity interest of the family convenient stores to my grandpa Willis. She remembers how strange it seemed that mom was suddenly always there. Mom would tell her how much she missed us, and that she promised that she would be a mom to us from this point forward. My mom was in agony over the situation she found herself in. She ultimately lost the house to the bank. She wanted to bring us to a better life, away from the turmoil in Washington. Although I was too young and not privy to a lot of these conversations, it helps me understand the source of a lot of my frustrations and misplaced anger in life, for lack of better words. I have a depiction of what a father should be. Unfortunately mine was never any of them. But like all of my siblings know, today, he'll be the first to admit that he blew it. I hope he will also understand the suppression of memories this has caused for me because the likeness of trauma associated with my abandonment that had already happened.

We finally moved to Hawaii. I should have been happy to be headed towards paradise. Instead, my heart had scabs all over it and I was just closing another chapter of life that had a really ugly ending that I had grown so accustom to doing. Changing my physical environment would later prove to be my outlet to try and make my internal pains disappear. Reset…reset…PRESS RESET! Help…me!

Lee Yong Yul;
A.K.A. Mark
Lee Owen

Mark and Sherri

VOLUME 67   ISSUE NUMBER FORTY-THREE   SEQUIM,   WA   98382
                                                                            1979

Brad Owen Reports

MARK AND BRAD OWEN

State Representative Brad Owen, D-24th District, brought in a high-powered lobbyist to testify before the House Judiciary committee last week on legislation he is sponsoring to grant foreign born, adopted children Washington birth certificates.

The lobbyist, who quickly won over the committee members and others in attendance, was Owens six-year-old Korean born son, Mark. The legislation (HB-4) is designed to make it easier for the foreign-born, adopted child to cope with government bureaucracy.

"Most foreign-born children, particularly those from Asian countries, have no birth certificate. The problem *is* government bureaucracy is not capable of understanding this fact of life."

Owen explained that the lack of a birth certificate has created problems for these children when entering kindergarten, applying for a learners permit to drive a car, obtaining a passport and on other occasions where a birth certificate is used for identification.

"The last thing an adopted child needs is to be pointed out as different when participating in the normal activities associated with growing up, such as obtaining a driver's license."

Owen said Washington had previously allowed the adopted to obtain a birth certificate, but the law was changed in the fifties.

"No one I've talked with can remember why the law was changed in the first place," he added.

The younger Owen said little during the hearing except to tell the committee his age and point out: "Brad Owen is my daddy."

Brad, Nancy and Mark with Governor Dixie Lee Rae

MEMORIAL CLINIC, Ltd., P.S.

DOCTORS MEDICAL MALL

500 NORTH LILLY ROAD

OLYMPIA, WASHINGTON 98506

TELEPHONE: (206) 456.1122

General/Family Practice J. M. Burkhart. M.D. Edward G. Laclergue. M.D.

Internal Medicine
Feme S. Focht. M.D.
F. A. Griesman. M.D. James 1. lux. M.D.
Owen G. Reese. M.D. Paul E. Sandstrom, M.D. James A. Thompson, M.D.

Obstetrics-Gynecdou Roger W. Carnes, M.D. M. R. Hunter, M.D. Wayne M. Parpala, M.D.

Pediatrics
Cole V. Mason, M.D. P. R. Vandeman, M.D.

SurgelJ
Thomas R. Hazelngg, M.D. Robert S. Hipp. M.D.
T. Reed Ingham, M.D.

Consulting Radiologists
C. W. Reade. M.D. Hendrik Stiggelbout. M.D. William M. Veatch, M.D. D. L Wishart. M.D.

Gerald L. Whitcomb Attorney at Law 103 South 4th Shelton, WA

RE: OWEN, Mark L.

Me: 04-44-20 #01

Dear Mr. Whitcomb:

Mrs. Owen has asked that I write you, sharing with you our evaluation of Mark. I have seen him on two different occasions, first in June, 1976, and again in December, 1976. The mother's main question related to his actual age, as he came to her with a birth date of March 5, 1971, but she wonders if this is, indeed, accurate. When I first saw him and he had recently arrived in this Country, I thought his performance was more like a three-year-old than a five-year-old. Certainly, his growth and development, as judging by our North American standards put him at that three-year-old level. His growth can obviously be influenced by food, degree of stimulation and environment and, indeed, background. This makes any estimate as to his correct age, of course, very difficult.

On re-examination in December 1976, he was doing quite nicely in his adaptation. Again, I felt, although his chronological age was six years, his performance at that time was more like a 4 1/2 to 5 year old. A bone age done then showed him to be 3 years and 3 months, but this is only an approximate estimation.

I think in conclusion, taking into consideration his bone age, as well as his need to adapt to our North American society, an age of approximately 4 years would seem appropriate. This takes into account his development, as well as his growth and his bone age.

Brad, Nancy, Sherri, Dana, Mark and Shanie Owen

The Owen gang and
the Harvard home

V

Growing Up In Hawaii

I remember when our plane was beginning its descent from the air; I was starring out of the little window over-looking the airplane wing. We were breaking through the clouds and my ears were beginning to pop. As the plane's altitude was getting lower and lower, I began to see the white caps of the ocean. There were a series of smaller Islands not too far off from my view of the large Island of Hawaii directly in front of us. Our plane was headed for an island surrounded by water. This site was pretty amazing to see. The ocean was becoming a really pretty bluish color. You could see waves crashing against the island as our plane got closer, and closer to a really thin, long cement strip in between a bunch of small hills, palm trees and as we got closer, really a bunch of lava rocks.

Oh my gosh! Hawaii! Paradise! The airport was so small we had to wait in the plane until they wheeled over a set of stairs for us to exit. The door opened and it felt like a heat wave. I was in jeans. I grabbed the railing and walked off the plane. Our next chapter of life was beginning to unfold in front of my very eyes. We were officially going to become members of YWAM (Youth With A Mission), a worldwide Christian training and outreach organization. The organization itself was set in Kailua-Kona, Hawaii, atop a small hill. It had an awesome view of the ocean, classrooms and lecture halls, a large feeding area for meal times, and temporary housing for families that would arrive from all over the world as they embark on their initial training that was known as a Crossroads or discipleship training school (DTS). Its purpose was to prepare them for their next journey in life as missionaries. The headquarters of this organization we were at was commonly referred too as the YWAM base.

During the day we attended the transitional private school on the YWAM base. The classroom had a volunteer instructor that would oversee assignments and proctor exams during their DTS training. The reality is that with little oversight myself, Dana, and some other students knew where the answer booklets were. You can say that any grade less than an "A" was unheard of. In the evening we sat in the pavilion area, which was a stage overlooking a series of fold-up chairs, covered from the elements of the weather, and no walls, to listen to speakers and have praise and worship seminars.

After six months when my mother completed her DTS, we were transferred mid-school year to the public school. That's where I met my new best friend, an outsider from Colorado. I also had my first Hawaiian puppy love. She was Japanese. The adjustment period wasn't too difficult. Two years of pres-school in the same location, kindergarten through half of 4th grade at the same elementary school, transfer to another school in Shelton, Washington to finish 4th and 5th grade, transitional schooling for six months on the YWAM base, and now the Hawaiian public school for 6th grade. Yeah, I'd say a new classroom was not too difficult of a transition for me.

I don't recall the specific time frame, but somewhere during this chain of events my mother married this Australian entrepreneur named Frank. He promised the world to her. He had a million business ideas, including a water purification system to convert salt water into fresh water. We moved from the YWAM base to a house with a pool and a view of the ocean in White Sands Estates of off Queen Kalama Avenue. Frank drove this really large, red, convertible that us kids would sit upside down with our backs on the chair and our feet dangling in the air. Frank hated this. It was always "don't sit this way" and my mom saying "its okay".

That neighborhood is where I met another new best friend. His family also took me in as their surrogate son. They would take us to pizza parlors along the ocean front, give us money for video games, while they would sit back and have a few beers. That was the first time I remember seeing people drinking in a bar. I was fascinated with what they were doing. That was a lifestyle that up until this point I had only seen on television.

I remember the neighborhood delinquent that nobody really liked. He was into dungeons and dragons and kind of weird. He showed me this empty toilet paper roll he had in had found in his parents room. In it was tinfoil covering a hole they had cutout. Inside the tinfoil were tiny holes and some green stuff. Apparently I was seeing marijuana for the first time. In Hawaii it's known as pakalolo. I didn't try it out of fear of crossing the line of innocent cool too social deviant. Oh, and the mom factor of course. Cold you imagine being so little, drugged up and being scolded by your mother? There is some safety in that statement though. There are so many kids today that live in a world that cannot produce this kind of fear from their parents. What would they have to do to make their parents stop and notice for a moment? Nonetheless my mind was really fascinated with this funny green looking stuff.

My mom's new husband talked about his mansion in Australia that we would someday visit once his ex-wife would quit trying to take all his money. He idolized his three kids that would be our new siblings. Eventually they would be moving here to live with us. In reality her new husband had us living in fear. We had to act a certain way, we had to sit a certain way in the car, we had to watch certain TV shows when he was home, we had to be a certain way in public. My little brother Adam said he found a humongous pair of underwear on the floor of my parent's bedroom. It had racetrack stains on them. Gross! Or maybe even funny.

During this marriage is the time I had my first entrepreneurial experience. Maybe influenced by him, maybe not. I setup my little sister Sherri's first lemonade stand. Her and the neighborhood boy even had their picture in the newspaper. However, I collected the money, made the sales pitch to all the joggers, even got them to tip. This was a really neat experience.

Nine months later they were getting divorced. My oldest sister Shanie says that Frank was threatening to kill us. Mom had found a briefcase full of unpaid bills in her name that he had been hiding. She had confronted him about it and we barely made it to the bedroom and locked the door. It was actually her that escaped through the sliding glass door and ran for help. She had to sneak back in without him knowing. We were still locked in the room when the help arrived and continued to stay there until after lunch time (with no food since dinner the night before). Finally she snuck into all the bedrooms while mom and Frank and our attorney whom she had called from the beach pay phone were talking. She packed clothes and toys for us kids, her clothes and mom's clothes, told each of us to take a suitcase and marched us out to the car. At that point mom joined us and we left. That was the last time I ever saw him. Unfortunately I later saw his daughter, or my ex-step sister for the first time, at a youth group function. I was frozen and so was she. I didn't say hello. I left and never came back. I didn't know how to process these feelings. However, I do know that my mind had already started to cultivate new ideas about life so many years ago, and none of which ever included the promise of a functional family.

This didn't help. After a zillion failed business ventures, another bitter divorce and now my mother is left completely broke and in debt. I remember hearing her talk about how he used all her money and maxed all her credit cards. We were really well off financially until we had met Frank. We went from being upper middle class to living in government subsidized housing as our place to call home. Oh, and the red convertible he drove, that was purchased with my mother's money as well.

So, back to the YWAM base. My mom began volunteering at the visitor center, which was officially known as the Aloha Center. My mom was very good with welcoming new members joining YWAM. Her commitment of time allowed us to offset the cost of food on the base. Things weren't okay though. And not like one of those butterfly feelings you get in the pit of your stomach that eventually subsides. I mean the feeling you get of sadness from the frustrations I could sense within my mother that she hid behind her smile. The feeling of powerlessness. Things aren't right. I'm starting to consciously miss my mother. I'm starting to miss my sisters, my brother. They were there physically, just not emotionally anymore. Was it them? Was it me? The daily reminders I was seeing in my mom's face were beginning to drive a stake into the feelings of pain. I wanted those feelings to disappear. Go away! I started to feel more and more sad as each day progressed. I wanted my father back. Where are you? Dad? I thought you were supposed to protect us? Is that not the role a father assumes? Is that not the role you agreed to when you "rescued" me from the orphanage in Seoul, Korea? How is any of this construed as "being rescued" now?

My oldest sister Shanie says that my dad never called us. That breaks my heart. She was the one that called him every month to ask him to pay the child support check that he was not sending. She knows that dad was very angry about the calls from her, but it was the only way our family could get him to do this. My mother could not afford any more attorney fees to go to court again for just one months support. This hurt my mother pretty bad. Shanie remembers begging my mother to let her call. My mom would say, "Let's just wait one more day, maybe it will come." After a while he finally started sending $200 regularly. Can you imagine so little being so much?

By this point in life there were a million things I was becoming very angry at. I was mad for being abandoned. I was mad at the family that rescued me couldn't make the decision to stay together. I was mad that we were in Hawaii. I was made that a new guy that pretended to be a father ripped us apart. I was mad at my mom for allowing this to happen. I was mad that we lived in government-subsidized housing. I was mad at the religious views being forced upon all of us through this organization that coincided with my mother's beliefs. I was mad that our family was becoming completely reliant on this organization for survival that my mother said the Lord had told her to join and volunteer as a way to provide for us. I was mad that I felt I had nowhere to ask for help. Fine! You win then! I'm mad. Is that what you want? However, this was all so pointless frustration for me. Does anyone or anything really hear these words form a small child? And where are you dad? Do people ever understand the effects of their decisions? Do they even care? Or is it all just me? Why can't I communicate these things?

The government housing and poverty was a constant reminder of my fear of physical safety that I had so long ago suppressed. What must it be like for a small child to have its basic necessities like food and shelter become compromised when they are abandoned? I was scared. I wanted help. I wanted to know it was going to be okay. I was beginning to act out. I was so frustrated, angry and tired of hiding behind my empty shell of a smile that I felt society was forcing me to wear. Otherwise I'm just an ungrateful, adopted child, right?

One evening we were having a family discussion. All I heard was poor, poor, poor. No child support…. But God will provide. I was so tired of the same old rhetoric. She doesn't understand that the two things, God and her religious volunteering, that she was leaning on for strength, were the two things I was becoming very angry at for causing so much denial in the reality that we were not okay. Can't we get out of this? I know, no child support check. Big deal. You know this. We can't rely on him to send us enough to support us. How much of this is really his role anymore though? Aren't you divorced? Does he not have a new family? He's gone! I can't continue to listen to the same poor me conversation any longer. Can't you just quit volunteering at YWAM and get a job?

I didn't actually say any of those things. I was too scared. But at this point my anger is beginning to build and turn towards my mother for choosing to keep us in this situation. I finally told my mother if she really loved us than she wouldn't yell at us all the time. That's not even what I meant though. Really, I could have cared less. I just wanted everything to stop. Great Mark. A million frustrations and this is what you choose to say when given the chance to speak? I wish I could have communicated each frustration and been helped along to understand. However, I vented wrong and now no more conversation at all. The discussion at this point was now over. What a backfire this was. Really, I just wanted my mom to admit that maybe, just maybe her god won't provide!

So no more hiding behind false perceptions. No false perceptions of money, no more make believe social standing. Nothing. I was nobody now. I remember telling my mom that I would get a job and use the money from my paycheck so we could move back to our old house. She said no. What I heard was that she was okay with us living in poverty, sacrificing our lives for her religious cause. I felt so neglected. I wanted out. I felt helpless and unable to protect myself. History repeating itself just like when I was an abandoned child. My mom would say pray. To who I would think? God? Are you kidding me? As far as I was concerned I was not going to pray to the god that put me here and is probably looking down laughing at mw right now. I think bitter would be an understatement at this point in my life.

It was only later in life that I learned that when we went to sleep my mother was working at a grocery store to make ends meet. I only found out because I woke up in the middle of the night and she wasn't there. She raised five kids by herself. She didn't claim bankruptcy and she paid every debt back that Frank incurred. She taught me integrity that I later disregarded, but always hung onto as a base for my character. She fought when the rest of the world left her alone. As you read this, "I'm sorry mom. There are things that I felt and will feel as these pages unfold. I'm sorry".

My mom has since achieved her vision of adoption though missionary work. She currently lives in Arizona with her husband, Terry, of the past thirteen years. They run an adoption agency that has offices located all over the world. Years ago when nightly news stations reported the abuse in certain third world orphanages; my mother was able to obtain the unedited tapes that these broadcasts did not show on television. My mother traveled to the orphanages and saw the conditions the children lived in. Since the report was aired, third world countries have since improved their care of orphaned children in their care. Furthermore, my mother's adoption agencies have prompted countries to change adoption laws throughout the world.

I think she is very successful at helping abandoned kids to find new homes. I love her. However, this does not erase the emotional neglect I felt by the lack of her being involved with me because of her global pursuit to save orphaned children. I know that her adoption agency was not incorporated until the late 1980's. However, it's the years of planning that I misinterpreted as her life with a better interest than myself. There were discussions I had with my siblings about this. It would cause great anger in me. I would stop. I would whisper only to myself, "Mom, save me first."

Her heart was for orphans. Her heart was motivated by the Holt International agency. Legend has it that Mr. Holt who started Holt International Adoptions, would wander the streets of Korea every morning looking into the dumpsters for abandoned infants. Such is the way and society that places us together and finds more information that we still cannot deny ourselves that in certain countries this is normal practice that is not talked about. While other countries deny any type of need or abandonment. Her heart inspired my adoption. I know her good intentions and life saving missions she performs. However, sensible thinking cannot erase where it hurts in my heart the most. Adoption for me cannot be appreciated until abandonment is closed.

I think my strong will, though at times left on the shelf, were instilled by watching the resilience of my mother facing her own life trials, tribulations and unrelenting defense of her faith, her God. Nonetheless my mom and I never talked deeper than a surface level my entire life. I never expressed my feelings about the divorce or anything in fear that it would devastate her feelings. We never practiced expressing feelings with each other, good or bad, we rarely raised our voices. It was easier to just absorb whatever my mom would tell us, whether she raised her voice or not. Our silence was our shield. My shield growing up and my shield throughout my entire life. But I can't deny the pains as I get older and it starts to hurt more.

My mother's life devoted to her religious beliefs never placed money as an issue to stop her from her calling or purpose in life. Although her adoption agency is incorporated as a non-profit entity, no one working with her, including herself, receives a salary or stipend from the adoption fees charged to adopting parents. She believes that children are not to be a commodity. Rather, her compensation is received through donations by individuals, churches and other organizations that pledge monthly support. This lifestyle is not for everyone though. Her volunteer efforts demanded time away from the home that caused unforeseen neglect. These choices consequently made our financial lives a day-to-day gamble. During these times I remember telephone calls to my father to ask please send us the money he owes. Those were about the only telephone calls I remember making to my father. Otherwise I don't remember spending a lot of time acknowledging the lack of my father in our day-to-day lives until we had to pick up the phone. What a painful reminder.

The lack of money and the real life threat of feeling physically unsafe due to our living conditions made me feel like I needed to take my security into my own hands. My mind was in survival mode, which unfortunately compromises a lot of values that I had otherwise been taught. Giving, kindness, tolerance, understanding, forgiveness... These values were placed on hold, indefinitely. I embezzled money for the first time. It was a candy bar fundraiser for the public school I was attending. Rather than the normal price of a dollar, I was charging everybody $1.50 and keeping $.50. I even remember talking with my friends about raising funds for fake walk-a-thons. Those never transpired though. However, the thoughts were definitely in action.

While my sister Dana and I were attending the public middle school. My oldest sister Shanie was attending classes at the public high school. She didn't like it. The Hawaiian public schools were famous as some of the worst schools in the United States. Kids were smoking marijuana everywhere, the teachers weren't teaching a thing, and there were fights constantly. She didn't feel safe being there as a white person. Asians weren't safe from the Hawaiians and so on. Racism was rampant. She left and completed almost two and a half years of home schooling in six months. Shortly after all of us kids were transferred from the public schools to YWAM's long-term private school. The classrooms weren't divided by age or grade; rather, kids from middle school through high school did their studies in the same classrooms. Initially I was relieved to be out of the public schools. I missed some of the friends I had made, but I got over it.

This started a new chapter in my life. We participated with Kings Kids. This was a function that was founded by one of the members of YWAM. It included youth leadership training camps and summer evangelical mission trips. Children and young adults would sing and dance in colorful costumes, while performing praise and worship in many different languages, in attempt to bring the word of God to everyone all over the world. During the summer of 1984, actually the first year after leaving Washington, we joined Kings Kids for the summer Olympics in Los Angeles, California. We would learn our performing arts at the same school the movie Grease was filmed at, remember Rydell High? One afternoon when we had some free time, I had climbed up the goal posts in the football field while the other kids played soccer. A ball was kicked and it hit me square in the face. I had blood all over the place. However, something, someone, kept me from being knocked off the goal posts. I will always remember this event vividly. I still remember the guy that kicked the ball. We closed the summer by performing in front of the Olympic crowd. What an experience to have as a child.

During the following summer I traveled to Europe with Kings Kids. I rode busses through, trains and ships through many of the countries. I ate hard, jelly filled bread, and did performances in front of the infamous mermaid statue in Denmark. I learned a few German words in Altensteig, Germany. I saw wooden clogs in the Netherlands and ate real swiss cheese in Switzerland. This summer was a turning point as some of my repressed feelings surfaced. As a 13-year-old boy, I missed my dad. I had a lot of feelings of disappointment, hurt and anger flowing within my heart and mind. A lot of nights I wanted to call him, I didn't. I talked with the founder of Kings Kids. We had a long, intensive session where he prayed for God to heal my heart. I talked to him as if he was my father. I told him how much I hated him for leaving mom. Leaving us. I cried tears from so far deep within me I could barely breathe. He held me in his arms letting me sob. That is the only adult male father figure I have ever been able to be held by. I finally looked in his eyes and said "I forgive you". As I re-write these memories through tear filled eyes, "I ask that my dad, my father will forgive me as I have forgiven him for the things I am about to say and do as you read the later chapters of my life."

As my summer In Europe came to a close, I had to board a plane to Washington State to reunite with my sisters during my dad's summer visitations. Unfortunately there were only three weeks left until I would have to return to Hawaii. In Hawaii and Europe my dad, or lack there of, was out of sight and out of mind. In Washington I had to face the painful reminder that his presence was only temporary. These feelings caused frustration and anger within me. I would get mad for being forced to be there. Then I would get mad for being forced to live in Hawaii. Then I would get mad for being in Europe and missing on my time with my father.

My sister Dana reminds me of some of the fun times we had during our summer visits with my father. Like the summer we learned to water ski. It took her almost two weeks to get up on two skis and I got up in two days. She was so jealous. This was the same summer Dana would fall in love with every high school boy that lived at the lake. We had another summer that we traveled through a resort in Montana, drove through some western states and ended our trip in Disneyland. That was a fun journey. A long car ride home, but a very fun time. The close of each summer was always a time of happiness and sorrow at the same time. Saying goodbye is awkward for me. However, I know it's time to leave and let my father return to his family, his wife and his son. The drive to the airport always seemed so long. Like I wanted to get there but I didn't want to leave. One of the trips I was able to stay an extra couple days or so after my sisters had left. I remember looking through the airplane window as my father waited for the plane to depart. I would always think to myself, I wonder what he is thinking right now? Is it work? Is it traffic? Is it the long road ahead? Or is it me? That trip I cried in the airplane chair. The stewardess told the lady sitting next to me that I was sad because I was leaving my father to return to my mother's home. The lady tried to comfort me and tell me it was okay to cry. She said crying wouldn't make me any less of a man.

YWAM had a gymnastics function that was started by another one of its members. The instructor went to Penn State, roomed with one of the former Seattle Seahawks running backs, and even coached several of the backup gymnasts for really the only major gymnastics movie ever produced. He was later asked to coach the men representing America during the floor routine in the 1998 Olympics. However, he declined the opportunity and followed his heart, his passion for God that included moving to Hawaii and starting the gymnastics division affiliated with YWAM and Kings Kids.

In my great quest for family a family structure, my gym coach and his wife became my surrogate family. They invested so much time and effort into my training. They were convinced I could receive a scholarship to Penn State and eventually compete in the Olympics. They were so committed that when my mother couldn't afford monthly classes, they would let me coach gymnastics to the younger kids to offset monthly dues and continue my training. The kids really looked up to me. I would teach them forward and backward rolls, back handsprings, parallel bar routines, ultimately training them to compete. I would sense their frustrations as I tried to teach them more complex routines. Their frustrations and inability to learn would trigger my own feelings of inadequacy. I didn't want them to feel inadequate. I didn't want to feel inadequate.

I remember my gym coach being so excited when I learned how to do the layout with a full twist in my first attempt. My mind is very powerful. I would visualize and accomplish many things in the gym. His instructions were planted in my mind. I knew exactly how each part of my body would work with each other as I was free falling in the air. The concept is to keep your body completely straight as your doing a back flip on the floor routine. The trick however was to add a full twist that starts by leaning towards your left shoulder as your flipping backwards until your feet are above your head. Then transferring your weight to your right shoulders as your feet return to the ground. He was ecstatic. While he was trying to spot me and soften the landing if I didn't accomplish the trick, all the other guys in my class all jumped to their feet in excitement. It took him two years to learn this. He had the largest smile. Complete excitement. I felt ashamed. I don't know why. Like I didn't deserve this. I looked at the ground. He grabbed my shoulders and told me what a great job I did. He had to physically stop me from walking away and say, "Mark, you need to learn how to take a compliment." My guards were so high I didn't even know how to share their excitement for the things I would later accomplish in the gym. I would never open my heart to embrace my accomplishments within the gym in fear of disappointment when I would fail.

I was becoming very good at gymnastics by this time in life. At age 14, I had the opportunity to go on another summer trip to Europe with Kings Kids. This time less performing arts and more focus on gymnastics. A few small obstacles to overcome before I could leave. Like the fact of having no money to pay for the trip. I remember standing in front of the church asking for donations. I remember participating in fundraisers. I remember having to call my dad to ask for airplane money. I remember my grandma and grandpa Schmidt sending me $1,000 towards the trip. I remember becoming more and more embarrassed about not having money.

The following summer we had the opportunity to tour five Asian countries with Kings Kids. I got to sign autographs surrounded by cheering fans in the Philippines, get stuck in the elevator and rescued by fire men in Hong Kong, and stare at the ground from the tallest building in Asia. My neatest experience was being the first person to do gymnastics on the Olympic floor in Seoul, Korea during the 1988 summer Olympics. A very powerful time in life for me. Chapters closing as others are being opened. During this trip my mother asked if I'd like to visit the orphanage that I had been adopted from. I wasn't ready. In fact the trip to Asia, and now being confronted to see the very place that caused me so much pain in my heart was to overbearing. I didn't go. I scanned the bible until I found a passage that convinced my mother I didn't need to go. What she does not know is the major trauma in my life it was resurfacing. I would stare from the building we were staying in and envision jumping off.

Throughout all these summer trips I met so many people. Got close and then watched them all leave my life. I made many decisions to stay surface level and emotionally distant from others to protect myself from feeling my pain of abandonment, as they would leave at the end of each summer. I could not stay hardened forever. Sometimes you have to be open. I developed a special friendship with one of the girls. I cried when the summer ended and we went our separate ways.

During the fall of my 15th year, maybe two or three weeks before turning 16, my competitive abilities finally awarded me first place in my division for the State of Hawaii gymnastics. I even had my name placed in the International Gymnast Magazine. This actually did bring some excitement for me. Maybe some bragging rights? After the state finals in Maui, I started feeling like I could actually do this. I wanted to try harder. I wanted to open my heart and become passionate about something. We set out a path to train for the regional competition in the State of California. This competition would include the best gymnasts from each of their respective divisions from the western states of Washington, Alaska, Hawaii, Oregon, Idaho and California. The winner of these events would compete for national titles and become a base of selection for Olympic contenders. Something happened though. After I turned 16, my gym coach moved his family to the State of Oregon. He wanted me to transfer schools and move with them to continue training. I didn't know if they were serious and never knew how my mom would feel. I never moved. I felt rejected. I lost my dream that I was starting to open my heart too. I shut down. This instant collapse triggered my feelings of abandonment and in-security all over again. The feelings of abandonment from my biological family were suddenly exposed. My mind said I told you so Mark. You don't deserve good things. Deal with it.

Despite these negative feelings, YWAM, Kings Kids and gymnastics is where I met my next round of friends that would be in my life for the next several years. With these kids I was able to travel the world and even participate in a walk on role during a Japanese version of Magnum PI. Although life should have been great, I was becoming so confused with my feelings of abandonment that would surface and I would push down. I was getting confused of living in Hawaii and then being whisked away to Washington to see my part time dad and his family, my step-mom and stepbrother. I didn't like being poor and I was starting to doubt God. I was looking for a place to vent my frustrations. I found one. Inside my anger, my life full of disappointments and broken expectations was being focused towards my mother. I began to think my mom's underlying intention for sending me on my summer missions trips were really to take away from the time I would have spent with my father. I started to question what the basis of the summer trips were. To preach the word of God? Hmmm. If God equals summer trip, and summer trip equals time away from visiting my father, and time away from visiting my father meant satisfaction of my mom's resentful heart, then I wanted out. Out of the whole thing. God, missions, YWAM, just let me go. I didn't show it though. I couldn't. Rather, I smiled, I laughed, and I participated.

At the tail end of gymnastics and performing arts with Kings Kids, my oldest sister Shanie left for Papua New Guinea for her Discipleship Training School. This was to prepare her for a life as a missionary, which she now does full time in Eastern Europe with her husband and three kids. I'm very happy for her and her family. Prior to her marriage she talked about this guy she met during her DTS. That's when I felt like I lost her; even though we had already began our separate paths in life, she was leaving, and this hurt. This reinforced my feelings of rejection and abandonment and made me feel alone. Just like when I was two and a half years old. I didn't know it at the time what feelings inside it was triggering. I just know I didn't like them. I pushed them down, just like all the other ones. But for how long could this last? Until I explode and say things I wish I could take back? I wish I did not vent my frustrations and anger on her. I wish I did not bottle up my feelings until I exploded. "Shanie, I'm sorry."

Before she left she had gotten me a job with her at a deli. That's when I left YWAM's private school and began home schooling. I worked for the last two years of my high school life. This seemed okay at the time given the choices I felt I had. My mother wouldn't let us attend public schools and we had to rely on donations to stay in YWAM's private school. We were living in sub-standard housing and I was getting to old to think this fantasy world was very realistic anymore. What about my future? I didn't take school very seriously anymore. I never studied. I looked up all the answers for all my tests, well, at least the from the answer books that my mom did not take with her to work (trickery!). Nonetheless, I graduated with a 4.0. Imagine? The translation of these events really made me feel like a high school drop out. Although I was invited to the junior prom, I missed out on all high school sports, dances, classrooms and development of social skills with children my age in a classroom. I was actually bitter about these choices. I just pushed these feelings down too. Remember Mark, smile, you like life, you're okay. Otherwise what reason would this family have to keep you? That is the reality of the translation of events and feelings from my mind as an abandoned child.

One night when we were at the deli waiting for my oldest sister and her co-worker to finish cleaning the kitchen area, I took $20 from the blue moneybag that had the contents from the cash register. The next day her boss confronted them. I remember my sister distraught for days. I never said anything. I didn't really feel too bad about it either, except when I would have to look at my sister. Wow, I think I could get away with anything if I put my mind to it. However, that is the only thing I took from them. I wanted the money but even more so I wanted the thrill. It was me I would say inside. Nobody knew. People are easy. What a great release of bottled up frustration.

Our work uniform was a flowered aloha shirt, white shorts and a red hat and half apron. Funny looking back. I liked the new journey in life though. I could start making money and secure my own financial insecurities. I later transferred to the little fast food hut and worked there with my sister Dana. I was earning what I thought were large paychecks. I started buying more and more material things to fill the impending void in my life. One summer we had a Japanese exchange student visit us (they used to every summer in Washington before the divorce). We always had fun with him. He would buy us lots of cool stuff. I remember once telling my mom if he bought me these clothes with the money that he was going to give to her, then I would give her money from my paycheck. I never did. I spent my paycheck on myself. I didn't even care that it affected my mom and all my siblings. My mom told me I was so self-centered I was like talking to a brick wall. I didn't accept this. Everybody liked me. In my mind my external act, or façade of happiness, was better than hers and therefore she was the self absorbed one.

My first two jobs covered about a three-month span. Then I ran into what I thought my opportunity of a lifetime. I was hired at a yogurt shop. This new yogurt store was the largest competitor to TCBY yogurt who owned the market of the soft serve yogurt craze of the late eighties. Penguins was being opened by Veronica and James, a Christian family that moved from California. It was a perfect job for all the YWAM kids. The husband was one of the former producers for one of the daytime talk shows. During the next two years I promoted to a supervisory capacity. I hired, fired, opened the store, did morning cash drops and warehouse yogurt runs in the company truck. More importantly I had established myself as a responsible person. I did it through the direction and guidance of my new surrogate family. I have a special place in my heart that will always belong to them.

Although confident, I was in constant search of identity. I adapted and absorbed personalities in all walks of life. If you were rebels, so was I. If you were God fearing, so was I. I developed friendships with another group of people. Mostly YWAM kids. Jake, Donny, Daniel and Michael. Each had a distinct personality that I absorbed as mine. Jake was Mr. Tuff, Donny was Mr. Kind hearted, Daniel was Mr. Identity and Michael was happy go lucky, I'm really only a 10 year old so watch me laugh.

Michael and I used to laugh for hours telling jokes to each other. We would record ourselves like DJ's on the radio. We even made surveys, polled the community and made a top ten countdown tape. AM 97. Why can't life always be this innocent? Daniel was a lot like me, the me that never exposed his inner self. He spent so much time trying to get people to accept him. He told me once that life is so hard having to be the guy that is always cheery. He said nobody would accept him if he showed them how sad he was inside. My mom had her reservations about him as well. She didn't understand why a guy his age would associate with people my age. Because of this it was very easy to take advantage of his feelings. One night I played on his insecurities. I told everyone at work to ignore him when he came into visit. We all laughed at his expense. He left crying. I picked him up as he walked home. I apologized and said we were all in on playing this prank and I had no idea that it would hurt you this way. That's a lie though. I knew. I wanted to see his reactions. I wanted to understand why someone would spend so much time caring what other people think. Could people really be that affected by someone else? More importantly could I? Are my feelings even real or are they just made up in my head? Nonetheless, I learned my ability to persuade people to turn against people they liked and how emotional factors would always play a role on the decisions a person would make. People were very shallow and impressionable willing to sell friendships. I was becoming a master manipulator. I just didn't realize what I was trying to prove to myself at the time.

During this time I really started to challenge my religious beliefs that I inherited from my mother. One of the photography stores in the strip mall was owned by someone who didn't believe in any sort of god. I'm not sure if that's agnostic or atheist. None of the YWAM kids were allowed to work there. We were even told to stay away from the store. The owner offered me a photography shoot and placed my photos on the wall of the store. I liked seeing me. It's proof I was here in this world. I told my mother what I did. I don't remember her response.

I didn't stop there. I pushed my doubt of religion even further. I remember driving back from a weekend youth camp with my little sister Sherri. I was tired and also questioning life. I told God I no longer wanted to live. If I had a purpose in life then show me. Otherwise, take me out of this cruel world. I was driving back at about 1am doing speeds of over 110mph. I was so tired it was very hard to keep my eyes open. I remember hearing sounds of the car crushing around me a feeling of flying. I remember hearing my sister saying, "Mark, what's happening." The cop later told me that my car flipped end over end and there were car parts covering a 100-yard stretch of the road. Too many things happened in that accident for me not to believe there is a God that wants me here on this earth. Bur for what? Even the way the car crumbling around us keeping us safe, including the tint holding the glass together around our face yet all the other windows were shattered. That fear was repressed until years later my sister told me she prayed the same prayer I did on the drive back.

My car accident was on November 9th, five days before the birth of my first nephew. This was another significant event in my life. My nephew Casey was born to my middle sister Dana. We had times growing up that we were very close. We shared a lot of memories together. However, the pains from my abandonment that were reinforced during the divorce hurt me real bad. I reacted. I lived life with a huge guard. It made always waiting for something bad to happen or for people to leave me. Consequently, I have large blocks of time that have been long forgotten. Sadly enough, many of those times were happiness replaced by sadness, then anger, and then memories all repressed. I do have a painful memory of being so mad and kicking her. I kicked my sister! I wasn't mad at her though, I was angry inside. I didn't even know how to communicate what I was angry about. She cried. A combination of these events is when I feel like we went our separate ways. I took on a lot of guilt and blame. I remember one night when she asked me why I never talked to her anymore, I didn't have an answer. Through no fault of her own I didn't know her anymore. I didn't know anyone emotionally anymore. "I'm sorry Dana."

Dana has since moved to Arizona with her husband. Two of her five beautiful children have a disorder called congenital adrenal hyperplacia. This disorder requires daily medications and frequent doctor visits.

I have to admit that prior to her pregnancy I was starting to get close to her soon to be husbands family. They are Hawaiian and have a large family. I felt like none of the locals would bother me because of my association with them. Dennis became a great friend for me. He was the older brother, a role model, someone for me to look up to. As the wedding got closer our time together diminished and I began to find a friendship with his younger brother Kaleo. He was always in and out of legal trouble. I went to a party with him that had booze. I never drank but my curiosity was growing. His bad boy image made him popular in a way that I had never experienced. Inside it fascinated me.

This was around the time I fell in love with the person I later realized was the last person I would ever give myself emotionally too. Her name is Alyssa. Her family were real estate developers that moved from California. She had a younger brother. She is such a beautiful person. She's half Italian, curly brown hair, and the most beautiful eyes that I could not stop myself from getting lost in. Inside she was the person that showed trust, care, kindness, compassion and understanding of the things in life that I was to scared to talk about. I loved her. She was my best friend during those two years. We went to movies, sang my first karaoke song with her family, shared my sister Dana's wedding together, and attended youth group events. I liked her because I could laugh and not have to feel my emotional pains inside. I could run in the rain, sing out of tune, laugh together just by being in the same room. I lost her after I graduated high school and moved to Washington to experience my first stint with drugs and alcohol. I clung onto her words for years. I used to re-read her old letters. She would always say, "Mark, it's okay to cry."

One time when a male friend of hers visited from California I felt very jealous. Angry inside. I felt I couldn't offer anything materially or socially to her. I was under-classed by her friend. I decided in my mind she'd rather be with someone like him than me. I started to pull away. The truth is he was just her friend, that's all. But this played very hard on my insecurities. I started chasing other girls. One that liked me but said guys like me were a dime a dozen. Another girl that was new to YWAM. She was a very bubbly person. Always happy. However, when all the dust settled I tried to get my best friend back. It was to late, she was already with someone else. I used the insurance proceeds from my first car wreck to buy a gold necklace for her. She went to California for Christmas and prayed and felt God told her not to be with me because there were things in life I needed to go through. I didn't understand at the time what that meant. I felt bitter and angry. Unbeknownst to me at the time, what I had to go through was the next 13-years of my life. As you'll soon begin to read.

Chapter closing and a new one beginning. My first drink of alcohol was when I was 17-years-old spending the summer at my father's house in Shelton, Washington. I met new friends that took me to a party. A kegger it was called. I had a beer, maybe two from the keg. During that summer I went to a few more parties, same level of drinking. When the summer came to a close, I stole a Heineken from my dad's store and packed it into my suitcase to take home to my mother's home in Hawaii. When I un-packed my suitcase I had a drink of warm beer. I didn't like it. I threw it away.

Returning to Hawaii from that last summer visit at my dad's house had changed me. I finally had a father in my life, I had a new step mom, a new brother. I would finally experience a full dimensional family. While I was there that summer I worked in their convenient store as a clerk for two months. I met new friends and started going to parties. I liked the party scene. I liked my new life. My father was a Senator and small business owner. He had social standing that fit what I was looking for. I was no longer a nobody. In my eyes my father was very successful. It is only during the next thirteen years that I would learn of his inability and my lack of willingness to communicate emotional issues with each other. It has me wondering what the meaning of success really is?

I spent my 18th birthday with all my YWAM friends. I cherished a card that I had received with personal statements from each of them. Most importantly, the one from Alyssa. I loved her but I was not equipped to show feelings or cry. I could never even begin to think that I could ever be there for her. She was in California when several weeks had passed after my 18th birthday. I packed my stuff to get ready to move to my father's house in Washington to start college. I cried over missing her for the next 13-years of my life, hanging on to every letter she ever wrote. Filling my life with people and women that would only hurt me more and more in punishment of not doing what I needed to do to have the very girl I wanted in my life for the rest of my life. I cry today as I let go of her emotionally, even though she's been out of my life already for so many years. As I re-read for the last time the words she wrote to me, "it's okay to cry". At 18 our lives parted and she went to a DTS class that focused on her relationship with God ultimately leading to her internal healing, I didn't.

I remember after I quit my job at Penguins to get ready for my big move. My brother Adam and I were having yogurt talking with the owner. Veronica asked if he was excited for me moving away to go to college. He said I guess. He was really sad. But I forced my feelings down and kept the conversation on me. My physical move was also my emotional move from my family, friends and entire life in Hawaii. I never even contacted any of my friends after I moved, except for Alyssa.

This move also represented my loss of my little brother, Adam. Although we shared a bedroom together we were never real close emotionally after the divorce. This move solidified his removal from my life. I just didn't know it at the time. I think back now to the verbal abuse I put him through, making him do pushups or make me lunch. He would never say no, even when he didn't want to, I used that against him. I use to rearrange my room and move the bed even with Adam sleeping in it; I thought that was so cool because he never woke up. The next morning he wouldn't know where he was. It's scary that even then I was tormenting people emotionally and not even knowing it. Taking advantage of my brother that lived a life in unfamiliar homes and then rearranging his surroundings while he was suppose to finally be in a safe home. "I'm sorry Adam. I pray you can forgive me. I also pray that you don't have to go through the same paths as I to find internal love."

My brother overcame a stint with smoking cigarettes, otherwise he didn't have to deal with drug, alcohol and gambling addictions. However, he has abandonment issues, signs of physical abuse from bad foster homes, and was sexually molested by his dentist. Today he lives in Olympia, sells wireless phones and was married on August 27th 2004. He's a neat man and I'm so happy that he never gave up on me.

This move also represented the loss of my little sister, Sherri. I have a lot of memories with her prior to the divorce. Like playing house and saving animals our cat would attack. After the divorce I have very few memories of my little sister. Sadly enough, few memories of most of my family. Today she is a college graduate married to an occupational therapist and living with her two kids in Arizona. She's such a great sister and friend to me today. "Sherri, I pray that you forgive me for the way I broke your trust while living with you and Matt in Seattle as I'll detail in the later chapters of my life."

"Dear mom, Shanie, Dana, Sherri, and Adam. Although I will leave and start a 13-year journey that exposes a dark side of medicating my internal pains. I pray that you will understand those things that hurt me inside and forgive me for those things that I have hurt you. I pray that you understand the path in life that I must travel to close my empty chapters of abandonment, in hopes that one day I'll be able to truly appreciate the family that I have and the person that I am."

DATELINE: Kailua-Kona-**Nancy Owen,** reports the non-profit corporation is now fully licensed by the state of Hawaii and can proceed with case studies on families who desire to either adopt or take foster children. Though babies available for adoption are currently scarce in Hawaii, Nancy said the corporation is negotiating and planning links with other states in the U.S. as well as other countries such as Thailand, Belize and Mexico. Immediate needs in Hawaii include adoptive or foster parents for children with physical limitations and emotional placement problems, and mixed ethnic back- ground, as well as older children, teenagers, and those who have been abused. Nancy said future plans are to add a full-time, free pregnancy testing and counseling center manned by trained volunteers who will help pregnant women work through the options of adoption or single parenting. For more information on foster care, adoption, or volunteering, contact Nancy Owen.

Photo: Dennis Fahringer

KING'S KIDS

Kings Kids in Europe

Korea 1988

Signing autographs
in the Philippines

Joshua, Gary,
Sean and
Myself

Harri's Deli and Penguins
Frozen Yogurt

Terra

My first totaled car

VI

College, Alcohol, College, Crime, College, Drugs...

I started the next chapter of my life living with my father, step mom and stepbrother Royce. I was working as a store clerk at their store, Brad's Quick Stop, and attending college as a marketing major. I met a number of new friends. Leon, Tyler, Jack, Taylor, Morgan and Jeremy. Although I thought very innocent I began a life of partying. Meeting new friends, dating new girls. Life was fun. I even participated in family events, but that didn't last long. Although I wanted the family setting, I didn't put forth any effort to be a part of their family.

One night I packed all my stuff in their jeep and moved to Olympia with Taylor and Leon. I didn't realize at the time the significance of this event. Moving out meant using my family as a safe place to go every time my life got to complicated. I didn't see it as using, I saw it as a family obligation that they weren't supposed to say no to helping me. They were supposed to always be there when ever I needed them. That's what my world led me to believe and I didn't even feel guilty about it, I didn't have really any feelings about it at all. My new living situation. Me, two roommates and the party house for college. I began going to school less and less, stealing beer, food, gas, cigarettes and money from my parents store to throw parties. That made me feel like king shit. Everybody wanted to know me. I slowly started smoking a little dope, going to clubs in Seattle. My drinking now was to get drunk. About 6-12 beers, four nights a week. Greed was consuming me. If I had, everybody wanted. I was the source of their fun, and everybody recognized that I was the person to know. Partying was expensive; I had to move back home.

The next four months of my life began a journey that unknown to me at the time would last for almost 13-very long years. While living in Olympia I started stealing beer, food and gas from my parents store. Stocking the house and showing up to every party with beer made me popular. My drunken nights became so important it consumed all my time and money. Despite the amount of beer I was already stealing, I could no longer afford rent, I could no longer buy food, I could no longer buy clothes, gas, afford my insurance. I started stealing gas and money from the till. I couldn't even make it to classes anymore. Although I was enrolled full time, I was only attending classes maybe 2-3 days per week, and that's being generous. I had an accumulated grade point average of .97. None of this mattered though. Wild parties, girls and booze. That's all I cared about. Our house was the party house for our college. I was it. I was popular, and a drunk, but I didn't care.

I worked the 2-10pm shift at my dad's store. One night the father of one of my childhood friends came into the store to buy some gas. They had heard I had moved back from Hawaii. They were really excited for me to hang out with my childhood best friend, Mark again. They said he needed friends. Several weeks later Mark was at the gas pump in an old, beat up blue station wagon. We talked for a minute and scheduled a night out. I picked him up and brought him over to meet my friends, and whoever else happened to be partying that night at my house. I had a good time drinking and catching up on old times. I was later told that he was weird. He was an outsider in high school. Nobody really liked him nor did they care too much about wanting to hang out with him now. In my small little mind, my ego was on the line of fitting in with my new friends. I wanted to be accepted and liked by everyone. I never called Mark again. Shortly after, his sister found him on his parent's couch. He over dosed on prescription pills. I couldn't even look at him during his open casket funeral. I had so much guilt. I felt like I sold him to fit in with my new friends. I felt for a lot of years responsible for his death. I shut my feelings down so I wouldn't feel the pain. He just wanted friends, and I wouldn't do that for him. The videotape they were recording at his funeral ended early. Even after his death they could not capture a full moment. Someone commented that it signified how his life too ended before it was time.

My life was starting to collapse around me and I didn't realize it. I moved back to my dad's house so I could re-group, get out of debt and get my priorities back. I just didn't know what my priorities were. I was dying inside and now the booze for the first time in life gave me perfect escape. A perfect escape from responsibility. A perfect escape from everything that used to mean something to me. My family, my friends, my school, my credit, my self-respect, my life. A perfect escape from all my pain. After my big move back home I started running around with a tougher crowd. Ones my first group wouldn't even associate with. These were people that stole, sold drugs, beat people up and had no respect for society at all. I started living another level of rebellion through them. I wanted to hurt people for hurting me. I wanted people to feel how it felt to be dead inside. I wanted people to feel the pain I was forced in life to carry. It was with this group I started experimenting with other drugs. I tried acid, marijuana, cocaine. The first time I tried cocaine we rocked it up and smoked it.

My obsession to fit in and please was at work and I fed it. I started smoking pot and tried acid to fit in. The head guy that the town was afraid of took me under his wing. I could do anything in that town because everyone feared him. A party he had that I was on acid ended up being the last telephone conversation I would ever have with the girl from high school that I thought I was in love with. That guilt sealed my emotional pain. From this point forward I would suppress my emotions indefinitely.

Shortly after, my uncle Cam was killed on his sailboat. His propane tank blew-up. The significance of this was not so much his death since we were never close, but the fact that I felt like my father vented his frustrations about the loss of his brother onto my shoulders because they couldn't get a hold of me. The only words that were said was how do you think the family feels when they can't get a hold of you, especially in a time like this. I felt at this point my father felt like it was partly my fault. I was very angry inside. Very angry at my dad.

Life in the party lane was so fast. I didn't care. I was completely indulged in this new identity and I wanted to experience every part of it. I remember a party the town bully, Joey, and I attended with two girls, one with a very jealous x-boyfriend. He tried to run us over in his car. He actually hit Joey and flipped him over the car before he hit a tree. I remember Joey getting up, pointing to the guy and saying "Now You're Gonna Die Mother Fucker!" He walked over and started beating him senselessly through the passenger side window. He wanted me to help. I was scared at this point. I slowly back peddled and stood with the girls. One said yeah, kick his ass, the other one cried begging him to stop. Joey was a golden gloves boxer; every party he was at it was a quest to show others how tough he was. Would this be his end? His end by the hands of Joey? We went back, got a gun but he was gone. He's now blind in one eye. I was never charged, the police arrested Joey for assault. I was scared but super intrigued. This guy was super human and would kill for me. My father and I would never talk about this except a mere mention of the fact of the arrest.

I wanted to try something a little more dangerous. I started selling pot. Not to make money, but to give the appearance that I was the big dealer. I financed most of it through a credit card and stealing cash from my parent's store. I would laugh, as people would meet me at work to buy dope. Some even trading for a little coke that I did lines in the employee bathroom. One night four of us were at Rainbow Valley. A hippy place that bands would play at and people would buy, sell and get high. I was in the mix. I was pushing gram bags and I went to my parent's jeep to grab more. There were to guys sitting on the jeep. "What the fuck you doing?" I sold them a bag and told them to get lost. The next morning I was taken in handcuffs from my parents store to go to jail. Holy shit, I was being escorted out of their store in handcuffs. I didn't really care though. I thought it was just part of the game, no real consequences.

When I got home my father threw me the phone and said "Why don't you call your mom now and tell her what a big man you are now!" I called my mom in the bathroom telling her how mean dad was being. She was right about him. She kept crying and crying, "What did I do wrong raising you?" I never internalized those words. I was mad at my father for being rude and trying to get my mom's attention. I felt lost and confused and didn't know how to express myself. We never communicated and the abandonment and the divorce left me feeling so lost and neglected. All I wanted was some attention. I never stopped to see their feelings. They were completely destroyed that their son was just arrested for selling dope. Reinforcement to them that they were bad parents. I never saw that. My father could have lost his jeep that night. The only reason they didn't seize it because I was driving it and it was in his name. I had blinders on. I just wanted them to say we know you exist. We haven't left you. We're busy raising all the kids and doing the best we can with the resources we had. I didn't get that answer. So it backfired. Instead of love and affection, it was pain and discomfort. I raised the bar.

I stole a checkbook that a customer left at my parent's store. I cashed two checks. One for $50 and one for $75 at the store. Then I went to a little convenient store in Olympia and cashed a check for $100 and bought a carton of clove cigarettes. I passed them out to everyone in college. Now I could brag about conning people and doing whatever I wanted. I was really becoming the bad boy. The rebel. In my mind that made me fit in. My preppy friends were starting to get a little scared of me but everyone wanted to know me. I could make anything happen. I played with people. How much negative behavior could I bring into their world and still have them asking me to be their friend. How many values could I get them to compromise for me? Big deal. They didn't like me; they compromised everything for what, a cigarette? C'mon. People were that shallow in my head. I finally was arrested for trying to cash another check at the same store. They recognized me when I walked in. However, they didn't know the checks were stolen, they thought my bank returned them for insufficient funds. So I left. They called the cops. I actually didn't get very far. I ran out the door and they chased me down. I stopped running. I was kind of embarrassed. I didn't really know why I was running. We went back into the store and waited for the cops to arrest me and book me into the City of Olympia jail. My first jail experience. I called my father to bail me out. I felt so humiliated. I again didn't acknowledge how selfish I was being. I never once cared how my family felt, or the effect that my dad, Senator Owen, had to bail me out of jail. I moved back home and the fact a criminal charge was pending didn't even phase me.

Okay, something different. Now my family is scared of me. Disappointed and confused. Afraid to talk to me. Wow, what I wanted so bad I was pushing further and further away. My playground needed to expand. I needed something, but what? So I reverted to what I knew. I started partying a lot. Became the life of the parties everywhere. You have a nice four-wheel drive, it can't go where mine can, and I would show them. Your girlfriend is hot, watch me go out with her, and I don't even like her. All the while I'm turning into a hater and all I wanted was love. I couldn't show it. I was smiling on the outside and dying on the inside. I had a small group of friends that were my base. Ones that I wanted to like me. Ones that I kept around to make me feel like there were parts of me that were normal.

While awaiting sentencing for these new charges, felony charges I might add, I stayed in school but quit working at my dad's store. I started a new job in the warehouse of a department type store. I was quickly promoted to the electronics department sales floor. I then spent three nights in jail in Shelton for the forgeries at my parents store and 60-days of work release in Thurston County for the forgery in Olympia and the drug sale. My father had to call my manager and tell her I would miss work for three days, didn't even phase me what he had to do for me. When my jail time was over I developed a new crime. I stole items that were overstocked in the warehouse and not entered into the inventory system. I had people return them later for cash. I also memorized the credit card authorization number that I later used to try credit cards frauds. This was also the time that I started maxing my own credit cards, buying expensive items to hide my insecurities behind. It took me a decade to restore my credit. Then I lost it again. Vicious cycle.

Now I really needed a change in scenery. Something to get me out of all this chaos. It wasn't fun anymore. I met a new friend named Larry. We had girls over for late night parties in the sauna at my parent's house. That's when I started trying speed, ephedrine pills and no-doze. This lifestyle was all heading into one direction. Larry moved to Bremerton with his girlfriend and I dropped out of school, quit my job of 11-months and moved in with my sister Dana and her husband Dennis' and their toddler Casey and baby, Savannah's house in Purdy. I didn't have a job. It felt good being out of Shelton. Behaviors didn't change though. I committed more credit card frauds. I started feeling like I could con anybody. I could talk any salesperson into letting me use stolen cards, even when I had to have them run purchases in smaller denominations for approval. I mostly bought a bunch of cool clothes and cologne.

I eventually got a construction job pouring foundations or new homes in Tacoma, Washington. It was to little to late though. I was pretty far behind on what little debts I had. My dad loaned me $600 to pay my bills and would drive from Shelton to Purdy to pick me up. We'd sit in traffic during rush hour trying to cross the narrows bridge. At 5pm he would pick me up and take me back home. I never paid him back for the loan or even thanked him for taking me to work. Instead, I used this as a way to ask him to let me use the jeep again. Really dad, it's better than having to drive three to four hours out of your way everyday. Linda was so upset at me. But they still did it. After a couple weeks I was driving again. Hurrah. No conscience at this point. All my pain was now my hammer. My ace in the whole, for lack of better words, to use against everyone else to get what I wanted.

My sister Dana and her family moved to Bellingham, Washington and had their second son Joshua. Wait, now I have to find a new place to live. I called Larry again since he lived only 20-minutes from Purdy. We started partying again. This time I had my first blackout. I started drinking in an apartment, shot-gunned beers and woke up the next morning on someone else's couch. Larry said they had to carry me home. Eventually Larry broke up with his girlfriend and we got an apartment in Port Orchard, Washington. This all happened in a matter of two weeks or so. Keep in mind during the in-decision period I was staying at Dana and Dennis's old place in Purdy until the end of the month. Everyday Dennis would call me trying to locate a final check that was supposed to come in the mail for him. They desperately needed money for food. I sat on it for three days trying to figure out how to cash it. I finally sent it to them. I'm not proud of this behavior. It's the way my life was. It didn't matter who I hurt. I couldn't feel my feelings. I would just sit there in self-pity, wondering why nobody cared about Mark. I was dangerously close to hurting people at levels that may become irreparable.

So now I have a wild idea. I need a new car. I trade in my dad's jeep for a new car. The deal was I had to give them $500 down in a week or so, and have my dad come up and sign the title over. Great. Larry and I started writing bad checks to buy cocaine. We bought a couple eight balls and tried to sell it to make some profit. After all, I needed money for a down payment on a car now. Isn't that a justifiable reason? We didn't really make any money. Nonetheless, we put a lot of miles on that car in the weekend I had it. Oh, I didn't tell you? I traded it in on Friday and on Monday I called my dad and told him I didn't want the new car. He made a couple calls and I got the jeep back. His thought was how could they trade in a car that didn't belong to you. And how could you trade in a car that didn't belong to you. My response. Chill. I'll pay you for what you think the jeeps worth.

So that was my weekend. Now I'm back to the construction job scraping boards and pouring foundations for new houses. I hated it. I quit. Time for something new. I wanted a cell phone. See, this is 1992 and cell phones are hot. You were it if you had one of those brick phones. They were like $900. All the new cellular companies sprouted and before I knew it, I was managing a store in Silverdale, Washington. However, I was only hired after I was rejected through about four interviews first. See, I have this gift. It's my ability to not hear the words no. I keep going until I get what I want. Then the chase is over, the excitement is gone. Always leaves me feeling empty afterwards. Kind of like being in a bad relationship. You like them but hate being with them. But better than being alone. That's what the chase to me was. Better than being alone with my thoughts, if I had something to chase. Dream land. Fantasyland. Surreal. I started trying acid at that point. Hard drug. It dries out your body and makes your joints ache. Try doing lines of coke, moving to acid, and then going to work with no sleep. It's not good for you mentally, physically or emotionally. By the end of my second week at my new cellular job I was not the same. Emotionally a wreck. I called my mom in Hawaii. I bawled my eyes out. Not on the phone, but after the call. I wanted to say sorry. I wanted to ask for help. I wanted to know why my life is so fucked up. I wanted to know why I didn't feel anything inside. Who am I?

Larry and I decided to go on a shopping spree. Unfortunately with my check book though. I called it in stolen and we bought everything. More clothes and lots of food. The one that got us? Chinese restaurant. Never write a check at a Chinese restaurant. They remember everything down to the part in your hair. Try getting out of that with the cops. Larry and I each received a misdemeanor. No jail time, just probation, I didn't care. Is there no end for me? That was Larry's final breaking point. Yeah, me too. Well, with him, not crime. I was bored and done using him. I moved into an apartment with a friend of mine in Olympia, Washington. I reenrolled into college, and reunited with the first group of friends I had when I originally moved to Washington. I started spending a lot of time with a couple girls from Shelton, Washington. I thought I was falling in love. I could never control my feelings for women. I either hated them or I was obsessively infatuated. I don't think the word "love" is part of that dictionary.

I got a new job now. A new start. I started bussing tables at a restaurant in Olympia, Washington. Oh, I also experimented a little more with acid and mushrooms. Too wigged out. I could watch people's faces melt. I could have 15-conversations with 10-different people in the span of two minutes. I could feel heat from the walls and then be overcome by the coolness of the ground. I got lost once. I went out to get some clothes out of my jeep. I turned around and didn't know where I was. I stood in the parking lot for what seemed like an eternity. My friends finally came out. They rescued me. I needed rescuing. This phase didn't last to long though. I stopped acid and mushrooms after a night I thought I was going to die. I tried something else though. Well, not all new things. I was drinking and went to a casino for the first time. An Indian casino out in Rochester, Washington. The grand opening for the first one in Washington. Wow. This place is amazing and it's filled with money. Although I lost $20 gambling, I made a mental note to come back. I finally found my new un-controllable rush.

I finally moved back home, again, and had my brother Royce screen calls for me. After 4-months, I decided I didn't want to bus tables anymore. This time in life I started to become very un-grateful. My parents would take us to Seahawks games and I'd complain about the seats. They asked me not to take the jeep stump jumping, I beat it up. Never ending list of ungratefulness. I subconsciously made it my mission to destroy everything that meant something to everybody. Destroy me, destroy you. That was my attitude. And yes, bored with my friends again. I needed new ones so I could absorb their identity and later blame them for my downfall.

I met a new friend named Matt. We were instantly best friends. Why? Common bond of emptiness and rejection. He lived in foster home growing up and was finally reuniting with his real mom. I could sense when people were open emotionally. That's when I would move in to be the hero and eventually bring them to my level of self-destruction. Difference is I always had a way out. I think really I felt I was sincere. I was just so ultra sensitive that I would open emotionally to these people. They would let me down in some of the littlest ways and I would turn to my destructive way. Killing with kindness. Matt and a few girls we had met would have all night parties at his parent's house. We would literally meet these girls driving down the road, talk to them at a stoplight, and have sex with them that night. My evil nemeses. I love women but hate how they made me feel. Jealous, angry, bitter and upset. And it didn't take much. One night one of the girls I met was dancing with another guy at a party I took her to. I left. I don't even know how she got home. I don't even know if was an old friend of hers. I didn't care. She betrayed me. She hurt me. Or maybe I hurt her. I never called her again. I didn't like the feelings of rage and jealousy growing in me. These women brought them out in me. I felt I had to hide them, just like my feelings in a closet.

Matt and I started smoking pot again. One night I bet Jack, good ol' Jack, the guy you could make do anything, a $100 he couldn't drink an entire half-gallon of vodka. He drank all but one drink. He didn't finish it and I didn't pay him. He got alcohol poisoning and could have died. I knew his insecurities. He was to easy. To easy to the point of boredom for me. He was someone I would call when I needed a ride, money or someone to hang out with when no one else was around.

So, back at the homestead I cashed a loan check in my father's name for $1,000. I kept partying and finally blew up the jeep. My father wrote me a letter asking me to leave. I cried. I couldn't understand why he was being such a jerk. I moved to Bellingham with my sister Dana again. But before I left I wrote down my father's and Linda's date of births and social security numbers. I received numerous credit cards in their names. I bought CD players, clothes, and cameras. Anything. Mr. Self destruct!

This proved to be a very frustrating time. Dennis and I got into Amway for a couple of months. One function we went to Portland, Oregon, I remember very vividly a spiritual experience. As I closed my eyes, I was lifted from the crowd and God said, "I'll never forget you". Forget me? I'm already gone. How can you love me? As we progressed with Amway, I started criticizing Dennis and even raised my voice to my nephew, Casey, once. He was sad and told my sister "Uncle Mark Mad". She explained I wasn't mad at him and then we were buddies again. I passed so much guilt onto him and still focused on my self-pity, poor me. That was one of the only few times I remember raising my voice to anybody. Even Dennis later apologized to me, which at the time I felt was owed. I used Dennis' soft heart for my gain. He even went nights without eating so we were all fed. Their car even blew up when I borrowed it for a trip to Olympia, Washington to party with my friends. I was so far removed from feelings of guilt, I didn't pay for the engine repair, nor did I feel responsible for leaving his family car less. Dennis never stopped trying though. He is a good man.

Dennis got me a job at a car wash that I excelled to a supervisor position fairly quickly. That's where I met another friend. His name was Danny. He was adopted. Perfect. I could see his insecurities from a mile awhile. He may have well just said hi, I'll be the one you use to fulfill crimes that you are too scared to do and then you'll coach me through talking with the cops so we won't get into to much trouble. Perfect. We stole credit cards and went on a forgery rampage. The detectives couldn't break him. I felt above the law. I was smarter than the detectives now. All things come full circle though. Trust me. You never get away, you only postpone. The owner of the car wash also owned a car stereo shop. I was featured in one of the commercials. It was pretty fun to see my face on MTV. And finally, I had a girl in Bellingham chasing me. It was hard to take her on a date though. One, I didn't have a car. And two, I was full of so much shame; I couldn't be the one to destroy her. Maybe a little bit of a conscience?

My new buddy and I were finally arrested for embezzling money from the car wash. The couple hours in jail was worth it at the time. The restitution wasn't though. We used the money to go to strip clubs in Canada where I had my first experience with a call girl. That was power to me. We could pick any girl we wanted as long as we had enough money. Drive up; wave them over and have sex.

Danny's wife had a delinquent brother. The three of us would turn up the heat a little more and go on a crime spree. Like what I was doing wasn't already enough. We broke into cars stealing anything we could find while writing hot checks so we could eat. I remember priding myself at how fast I could break into a Volkswagen. One birthday my family came up and gave me a golf bag and pull cart. My dad smirked about whom I stole my snowboards from. What? I didn't steal these. I was offended. I embezzled the money and paid cash, at least for one of them. What would possess him to think that I stole them? Hmmm. I was so cocky though. Once time I remember we pulled someone over and pretended we were the cops. We frisked him, made him stand with his hands on his car as we proceeded to steal his money and pot. I could have gotten killed. How stupid. My head though, nah, people are just my pawns in this game of life.

After I lost my car wash job of about 12-months, Danny and I started an auto-detailing business. I was very good at the public relations and marketing. In the first week we had a huge shop on a used car lot and a clientele list from my brother in law's timeshare job and the new athletic club, where we could also use their space and work out for free. The athletic club was a great place for us to break into cars. Nobody brought in purses and wallets into the gym. I prided myself because there was such a problem with cars being broken into, and they never even suspected us. I was lying and living a life of deception so well. That escalated my game of manipulation to another level. I know needed new types of personalities to try out. I needed more complexities.

During this phase both of my nephews' disorders were progressing. So, Dennis and my sister Dana moved back to Hawaii. I spent the next few months living in four different houses, chasing much younger women and wrecking two more cars. My life was so out of control, I actually felt my emotional pain for the first time in years. I bought a six-pack of beer one evening. I sat in my shop, crying in the dark, drinking my beer wishing I could have my dad back. He's gone. I alienated myself from my entire family. I hated them for loving me. I don't deserve love. Shortly after, I spent my 21st birthday on stage with a band call Skankin Pickle. My friends and I partied like a rock stars that night. A few days later I sold my car to a pawnshop and Danny, his delinquent brother-in-law, and I left for McCall, Idaho. It was snowing over the pass and it took us 11hrs of driving time. I was done with Washington State. I wanted to become a professional snowboarder. Idaho is full of snow.

In Idaho we partied. We went to bars and hustled money playing pool. We met a ton of new people and were the talk of the Town. I wrote bad payroll checks to myself from my closed business account for cash. I needed food, right? I also took people to stores and showed them what a rush it was to shoplift under the watching eyes of security cameras. Outsmarting them was my game. One night we had a party in our house. We invited the guys from McCall, Idaho and their rivals from Boise, Idaho. That evening we broke into one of the cars stealing wallets and car stereo equipment. The next morning, I un-plugged the phone from the wall and everyone went into town to file a police report. Why, the phone was working of course. The guys from Boise thought it was the McCall punks. In the mean time Danny and I headed for a hotel in town to get away from the chaos. Need to think. I received a phone call. The girl at the front desk liked me. She said the cops were on their way. Knock, knock, knock. Wow, police detectives, guns drawn and I was face down on the ground. I thought, what a joke. They must be really bored here. We spent 180-days in a low security military rehabilitation boot camp detention center for that crime. The first month I was in the dorms secured by a razor fence. They shaved my head, made me wear army wore fatigues and forced us to do daily pushups and march to military songs.

I was finally re-classified to the minimum-security side. Separate dorms on the hillside with no fences or locks. Kind of like a summer camp setting. I spent my 22nd birthday on the first day of a substance abuse inpatient treatment they offered there. Unfortunately, I knew at the time I volunteered for this to help me kill my boredom. I even became the tutor in the school. I got out of the fatigues and into jeans. Now playtime at boot camp was over. Time to face reality. I was extradited from Idaho through Oregon back to Thurston County to take care of my felony forgery warrant that I skipped town from Bellingham, Washington. Oh, I forgot to mention. Leaving Washington for Idaho was also to get a way from my felony arrest warrant. My final days of jail were memorable. I was made a trustee in the jail and helped in the laundry facility, swept and hung out in the kitchen. I slept in a dorm style area in the jail away from the regular population and was able to wear sweatpants and t-shirts instead of the orange jumpsuits. This made the 30-days go by really fast. I had only one physical altercation while incarcerated. One of the guys that was in custody for domestic violence picked a fight with me. He was hitting me. I just put him in a headlock until he couldn't move his arms anymore. The worst part is that I became very angry inside when I saw my dad's face in this man. How does this happen? They moved him to protective custody.

After about a month I was released. It's now January 1995. I'm 22 years old. I have a very extensive criminal record in Washington and Idaho. I've been incarcerated in jails in the Cities of Olympia, Bellingham, Shelton, and Thurston County, all in the State of Washington. I've been in the jail at the city of McCall and Boise in Idaho, a military boot camp rehabilitation program, one inpatient chemical dependency treatment center, and a brief stop in the jail in Portland, Oregon while being extradited back to the State of Washington from Idaho. I don't think crime pays.

VII

Reconstruction

In January 1995 I was scheduled to leave jail. Freedom for the first time in eight months, since I was incarcerated at a military boot camp rehabilitation center three states ago in May of 1994. My parents had a dinner function on the night of my release. They picked me up, bought some clothes and off I was, back into the real world. It wasn't long after being home that my parents helped me get a job at a construction company, again. Thanks. I started as a general laborer. I didn't have a car at the time, so I would drop my father off at the State Capital, dig ditches and sweep streets, then pick him up and go home and literally die from physical exhaustion. I was so out of shape the labor work killed me. It took me my first three weeks to be able to work without feeling like I was going to keel over from pushing a broom.

My typical day included work in the morning, and hanging out at my dad's office after 5pm, waiting for him to leave. In January, February and March I was at the mercy of the legislative session. Therefore, I was putting in some long hours. I didn't mind though. It's not as if I had such an intense schedule. Work, pay bills, and hang out with my brother Royce. Reuniting with Royce was a very neat time for me. I always wanted to bond with him. During our summer months we always had so much fun together. Working at my parent's store, building speaker boxes for the jeep, putting constipation medicine in his cereal, just fun, happy memories. The challenge with Royce is that he is my brother, as is Adam. I felt I had to choose one or the other. I ended up rejecting both. I hurt them in ways that no brother should. Not showing up for birthdays, only calling for money, and leaving them when they looked up to me the most. Why? It was already done to me by life. By my biological family. My culture. Everything.

So, I finally had to fess up to my parents. I had one last unresolved legal matter in the City of Bellingham, Washington. Before I left the State, I went on a rampage writing checks that I didn't have any money in my account to cover. Hey dad, well, I, ummm, well technically, I have a warrant for my arrest. My father made some phone calls and we were headed for court. The judge exercised some leniency and placed me on probation until several thousand dollars in restitution was made. During the next year, I put every dollar that I earned towards the money I owed. I paid the thousands of dollars in credit card debts I forged in my step-mothers name, I paid the one or two thousand dollars of restitution for the money I embezzled from the car wash in Bellingham, I paid the thousands of dollars in NSF (non-sufficient funds) checks, I paid 95% of all my collection debts.

I needed to something to focus my energies. I picked up a new hobby. I started writing. I love to write. I love creating characters and worlds to live in, even if only on paper. I had some neat concepts for some books where I would create the characters and plot. Then stop. Towards the end my writing, my bill paying, my work ethic, my drive were all compromised. I started drinking a little bit, and then spending money, a whole new set of self-defeating behaviors was on. I'm just not sure which order these events came, reduction of ambition and drive, or drinking and partying. My work schedule now included an hour at lunchtime at the local bar drinking and playing pool. This after I was promoted to the landscape foreman position where I essentially supervised a crew of about 3-5 employees. One evening after work a co-worker and I smoked some marijuana. I got so high, the term used when really the oxygen is cutoff from parts of your brain, major dopamine is released, your body becomes jello, your eyes literally close, and you become suddenly stupid and unable to do anything without laughing like an idiot. Kind of like inhaling a helium balloon. Only 100 of them without the voice over. I could barely see. I drove home hitting sidewalks in town and swerving all over I-5. I went straight downstairs to bed. No shower, no dinner, just sleep. My world was spinning so hard. It would be years later that I would ever smoke any pot again.

It wasn't long until I was in my fourth car accident. Sorry, I skipped the details of two in Bellingham, Washington, but you get the idea of my life thus far, right?) I was driving a 1990 white Ford Thunderbird. After a heavy night of partying, I took my friend home from Olympia to Matlock, Washington. It's a long, dark, windy road that's not very well traveled except for the loggers during the day. I fell asleep at the wheel. My car drove off the road, hitting a ditch and rolling over. The speed of the car hitting the embankment shattered the driver's window as I was ejected through it. The forward momentum threw me from the car into the ditch as the car rolled and landed on top of me, pinning me to the ground while I was wedged inside the windshield area, with my car upside down in the ditch. My legs and left arm was pinned under the car while my head barely stuck out of the windshield area. Really, the only place it could have been without being crushed. I could only move my right arm, which had blood draining down my hand and forearm. When everything stopped the only noise was the music from my car stereo. I couldn't even move to turn of the music. I don't remember exactly how I felt at the time. Mostly numb, in shock and wanting the music to stop.

A car pulled up and the guy jumped out screaming and yelling. I asked for help and he freaked out. He thought I was dead. I told him I was afraid of getting in trouble for drinking and driving and asked if he'd use a jack to lift the car and pull me out from under it. He said he had a warrant out for his arrest, but would call the police when he got home. He couldn't stick around and get arrested. It's funny the things that become important to you while in s traumatic event. I'm pinned under a car, bleeding profusely and I'm more worried about the police showing? Isn't that what they do? I guess I was in a little more shock than I thought. He was nice enough to turn the CD player off for me. That was the only car that drove by the entire evening, well morning now.

I don't remember how much time had passed. I think I was slipping in and out of consciousness when I noticed lights from the police cars, fire truck and ambulance. I heard some talking and one of the emergency crew said he could see my head and he thought it was severed from my body, which was pinned under the car. I opened my eyes and started talking. There were lights and people all over the place. The police officer told me they were going to try lifting the car off me with the Jaws of Life and pull me out. The hydraulics lifted the car and I could feel blood rushing to my legs and left arm. Then the car would crumble around me. That started to throw me in a panic. For the first time I thought I was going to die trapped under the car. I didn't cry, but I was squeezing the officer's hand so hard. I asked him if he would call my dad. I think I really thought my time was may be up this time and I wanted to say goodbye or something.

Things became a blur again and the next thing I remember was a tow truck lifting the entire car off me. I was pulled out from under the car and placed in an ambulance. I woke up in a hospital bed. My step mom was crying, my dad was just looking at me and my little brother Royce was expressionless. I had bandages on my left ankle, my left bicep and right hand. Three places where my skin was punctured yet no veins, arteries or bones were broken. Later in life, I would do some research and find out how fortunate I was to survive that accident. Apparently 95% of the people ejected from a car are killed. Of the remaining 5%, there are countless injuries, internal and external. I more or less walked away after being bandaged up.

A few weekends later I was at a party and my friend who was a local radio DJ said he had chills reading that report. He was live on air going through local news and the main story was my accident. He read a single car accident where the driver was ejected from the car and taken to the emergency room. The hospital verified it as Mark Lee Owen of Shelton, Washington. Then he stopped. He didn't know if I was alive or dead. He said it became very morbid and he felt like he was reading my obituary on live radio. I wonder if I should have stopped drinking at this point?

So, once again I have no car and a very bad partying bug. What to do. My boss at the construction company gave me a company truck to use and I got a night job at a yogurt/coffee shop so I could start

Suffering In Silence

By Mark Owen

saving for a new car. Unfortunately, this escalated my inside connection to the downtown party scene. I started dating a new girl, partying with new people, and life was good. It didn't last very long though. My insecurities started playing me hard. But another of life's little bailouts that I had grown a custom to was just around the corner.

VIII

College...Again!

I look back and it was months prior to my car wreck that I had already began a new journey in my head. I was bored and tired of just going to work and paying bills. I wanted more excitement. I started going to the clubs. Becoming the party guy was fun. New people, loud music and girls. The new girl I was dating was actually really neat. She was a couple years older than me and had a beautiful little girl. The first time I stayed at her house I freaked out because she had the same funky couch and chair that I used to own in Bellingham, Washington. I never told her that. Funny how many commonalities I would later find between the two of us. I was falling for her but I wasn't capable of love. I knew that about myself. She and her daughter made think of me, the little boy that missed his mother that had been gone from my mind for so long. Feelings were coming up that became overwhelming. I didn't know how to process them. Our phone calls became less and less until we finally separated.

Shortly after my dad arranged an internship for me with the Washington State Auditor's Office (SAO). Outside of the things I heard about my parents being audited years ago for miss-understandings by the IRS, I had no idea what an auditor was, or what they did.

Nonetheless, I was done working construction, done going to the clubs, done hanging out and drinking beer. I was ready for a change. A new goal, otherwise, I couldn't see what the point of continuing in the direction would be anymore. Why else wouldn't I just drink and party? Oh, maybe because it's irresponsible? I remember my job interview. I was all excited. I showed up in a pair of jeans, t-shirt and my long hair that was all one length just down to the bottom of my chin. I listened as the Elected State Auditor's Chief of Staff explained the job to me. If nothing else, he said, it would make me very marketable when I graduated from college. I was so clueless at the time; I didn't even stop to notice I was being interviewed in an office occupied by suits. No one was wearing jeans and t-shirts, just me.

I was offered the job and scheduled to start Tuesday 8am January 2nd, 1996. Of course I was excited, shocked and really pleased with my interview skills. Okay, I guess the job was already given to me prior to the interview, I just didn't know that at the time. One of the conditions of employment was re-enrolling to college as a full time student, and switching my major from marketing to accounting. Easy! Well, except for the fact that in my previous attempt at college I had already failed math 99 twice, talked my teacher into letting me try math 101, despite not meeting the pre-requisites, and failed that class too. Then I tried math 103, which was business math, because I thought it would be a more simplistic type of math. There's really no such subject, math is math. Like building a house each equation starts from a basic foundation, I just never took the time to learn the foundation. Oh, I failed that class too. I might have had a chance had I gone to class. But accounting, I could do this. The only accounting type class I had up to this point was a basic bookkeeping class (OFAD 135) that I barely earned a "D". However, in my mind, it meant I could pass and therefore, I could succeed as an accountant.

So I took my accumulated GPA of .97, switched my degree, started working full time during the day and doubled up on night and weekend college classes. I re-enrolled in many of my previously failed classes at the community college in Olympia, Washington, so I could keep the higher grade for my transcript. I transferred to another community college in Tacoma, Washington, to complete pre-calculus and business math, my evil nemeses. I graduated with my associate in arts in 1997. Only seven years after I initially started. Not bad, I was on my way. On to the big leagues. I had a tough decision to make. I knew I wanted to keep my job in Olympia, Washington and be close to home. I was looking at either finishing my remaining two years at a liberal arts school that was close to home, or attend a private Catholic college that was oh, four times the cost. I chose private Catholic School. My father telephoned the College President and arranged a luncheon with their lobbyist. I submitted my paper work and surprise, surprise, I was accepted for school. I was so committed to succeeding that I doubled up, and had all my classes scheduled out for the remaining two years. My priorities seemed to be in order, that's if graduating ahead of schedule were the goal.

My typical day started with my alarm at 7am, work from 8am to 4:30pm, classes from 5pm until about 9:30/10pm and a one hour commute home for dinner and homework. I was fortunate that my parents gave me a nice little car for school. Remember my never-ending car issues? That allowed me to use every paycheck towards the remainder of my past bills. During this time I was so busy that partying was rally non-existent, my work and school were my life. I was so focused and determined to graduate and make-up for lost time. I remember my first day of work in January 1996. I was sitting in the cubicle looking at all four partitions thinking this is it. This is the rest of my life. What a trip. Mark, happy go lucky, carefree, good luck getting any kind of a commitment out of him, too shirt, tie and an actual work schedule, that someone would notice if you weren't there. Really though, I didn't even know what an auditor was. My first few days were spent reading manuals just to find out what the heck my job entailed. Without too much detail, I think I can safely summarize the duties of the Washington State Auditor's Office. It's the independent branch of State Government that performs legal compliance; financial statement and federal grant compliance reviews of state agencies and local governmental entities. Independent? I was always confused about this, as I too was a state employee.

My first couple months of employment, I participated in small projects on the Technical Service team (Team TS). Around late summer of 1996, I began audit projects as an intern for the Financial Management Team (Team FM). The experiences were really exciting. I rode along to see the inside of under cover sheriff operations, locked in several vaults to count cash, and got to see the inner working of policy development for the major state agencies, that as a whole operate all the social services the state offers to its citizens, like food assistance, clothing, shelter, roads, etc. Really invaluable experiences. I seemed to be getting a pretty good handle on life by this time. So much that I thought I should get my own place. My father co-signed for an apartment in Olympia, Washington. I was 23 and living really, in my own place without parents or roommates, for the first time in my life. I was juggling work and school and my independence quite nicely. During my last quarter of school, I had transferred to Team Olympia. This was a local government audit team that had audit responsibility of all local governments like schools, counties and cities in Thurston, Grays, Pacific and Lewis County. As an Intern and under the assistant audit manager's direction, I led my first audit, A small school district in Grays Harbor County.

Independence has a price though. It means that when I make my decisions, there would be nobody around to place blame if there were negative consequences. Just me. I started partying more. I was hitting the downtown club scene. I bought an over-priced, handmade home theater system. Booze, electronics, clothes, and now rent. Yep, already spending more than I made. Not bad for one months freedom from the safety of my parents home. One evening during one of my parties, my brother Adam was so disgusted with me he got up and left. He thought I was a complete jerk while drinking. Arrogant, irresponsible, and not to mention a filthy loud mouth! Well, what else would I be with booze? What I didn't do is stop long enough to realize how much he looked up to me. He didn't like parties. He didn't like booze. He tolerated these because he felt this was the only way he and I could be in the same room together. Does my self-absorbency ever end? I slept with his date that night. Don't even imagine. A chemically affected mind will do things to meet its immediate needs. Even at the expense of his own brother.

After two months on my own, my brother Adam moved in with me to help pay rent. I wierded out. I made him a room in the dining room area, which although spacious, it wasn't a room. I constantly nagged at how messy he was. He left dirty dishes out, clothes, whatever, you name it was left out. I look back and it was almost as if I was ashamed of him. I don't know why. He's my brother, I love him. Years later I would explore options to find out where some of this anger inside was coming from. It was the Asian culture that I denied ever being myself that I saw in him that I was angry at. A constant, vivid reminder of the culture I hated for rejecting me.

Shortly after, Adam, Royce and I moved into my parent's old house. My spending habits got even worse. I was buying more clothes, more stereo equipment and more booze on the weekends. I threw lots of parties and my experiences with women got worse. My spending became so unmanageable again. At one point I had to sell my beloved TV just to pay rent too my parents. Wow! I remember being so mad at my step-mom. She is so unfair making me pay rent every month. Geeze, what world do I live in? Well, at least I had solace that I was still excelling at work and school. But for how much longer could I be self-destructive in my personal life, and try to counter its negative effects with external success in my professional and college life, before the two worlds would collide?

As the dust began to settle, I finally graduated college. Although horrible in my first round, second, third... of school, this time I doubled up on the classes and managed to graduate on the Deans Honor List, Magna Cum Laude with a 3.68 grade point average. I had finally completed a mission that I had set out to accomplish three years prior. My final attempt at college netted me a baccalaureate in only three years. Not bad considering only three classes from my previous attempt were transferable. All this while working and excelling at my full-time job. Finally! I remember thinking to myself, eight years for a four-year degree, I'm a real over achiever. Wait, say that again, eight years for a four-year degree. Over achiever????

My graduation unfortunately was not a shameless, guilt free acceptance of the keys unlocking a magical world that was waiting for me. Rather, I partied like a rock star right after finals. I started the booze after my final evening class. Barely enough time to put the pencil down before I had a drink of alcohol in hand. My classmates and I went to a bar in Tacoma, Washington. Danced and drank with a bunch of college buddies. I drove the one hour-long commute home after the bars closed down. I was so drunk a friend of mine called me the next day asking why I took the college exit in Olympia, Washington, which was 30-minutes from where I needed to be? She followed me to make sure I made it home. To this day I don't remember driving past that point or taking any exits. All I know is that I woke up in my bed. Another blackout of memory caused by alcohol? Probably.

Nonetheless my parents were so proud. Their son, the proverbial screw up finally achieved college graduate status. They hosted a party for me in their home for my friends and co-workers. People had so many nice things to say about me. Tons of gifts and food. Wow! We played pool and I drank wine. Really the first time I had had more than a sip or two in front of my parents. But I had to reward myself by getting drunk. I was getting out of control. I spilled wine all over the carpet and wall next to the pool table. Around 10pm my friends and I stumbled down the driveway to my house (my parents old house I was planning to purchase now that I graduated). We partied all night. Loud music and a new wave of people that showed up around midnight, I remember my father commenting on that. It's amazing that your friends won't even go to our house for your graduation party. They had to wait until the party moved to my house. Although my party after graduation party ended hours earlier, at 8am my father called and said that he received phone calls from neighbors across the bay who said my loud music kept them up all night. He emphasized that is not adult behavior. I got up, closed the French doors facing the water, and shut off my stereo. I guess the music was kind of loud still. And yes, I was still pretty drunk.

Nonetheless, although excited to graduate, I no longer had the goal or a hammer, for lack of better words, to give me reason to continue with the "good" path in life that I was on. I was suddenly faced with the useless feeling that I had nothing to do with my life. No more school, just work. Was that it? I wanted more. I suddenly felt without purpose. As if this feeling of uselessness wasn't enough, my grandparents tried to bring a cousin we had never met back into our lives. She was the daughter of my uncle that died after his propane tank blew up on his sailboat. I shut down. I didn't show up for the event. I avoided probably 20 phone calls from my grandfather, which only added too their pain of the loss of their son. All I could think about was my pain. I already went through too many times of temporary family members in and out of my life. Too much emotional pain to add more. I couldn't understand why they couldn't see how I felt. I was very bitter towards them.

So, I was offered two positions at work, one with Team FM and one with Team Olympia. I selected Team Olympia. Why, because audit budgets were smaller and included legal compliance, federal and financial reviews on each local entity. Not just legal compliance reviews of state agencies that I had performed for the past year and a half for Team FM. Because of my experience gained at this point, I was hired at a higher level than a college career graduate. I was hired as an assistant auditor II position rather.

Despite the professional success, I made some decisions that I later reflect back and see how damaging those were for me. I left the nest. I traded in the car my parents gave me for a little sports car. Used car, but nice. Basically, it was a street legal racecar. So now I had a car payment, but it would be perfect for picking up women at the clubs in Tacoma, is what my head was thinking. As if traded in a very nice, free car for a used car with a monthly payment wasn't enough; I also decided not to buy their house I was living in. After all, would you? Let's see, it over looks Oakland Bay, has a sauna, a full-unfinished basement, two bedrooms and a Jacuzzi, at a price well below its value. Oh yeah, I made the right choice. That's if irresponsibility was the goal.

IX

My New Career

I moved from my own home in Shelton to eventually renting a room from John and Chris in Tacoma. These two guys lived and breathed the Seattle, Washington party scene. They had lot of girls that they associated with and I wanted to really indulge myself in this type of lifestyle. I wanted to live the fast, party scene again. The first day I moved in to their house they brought out a tray of cocaine and placed it in front of me. It was now the summer of my 25th birthday; the first time I had cocaine in over six years. I was hesitant but I snorted anyways. The first line hits you from the top of your brain to the bottom of your toes. By the time you're done inhaling through your nostrils too get the chemical in your system, your dopamine is already on super-release mode. Your pupils dilate, your fingers, toes and the entire inside of your body goes numb. Imagine the feeling your body gets during an orgasm? Multiply it and you'll get the idea. You lose all inhibitions and all you want to do is talk and solve life's problems, but not in a negative way. You have all the answers. You listen to loud music, so you can feel the bass intensify your body numbness. We partied like rock stars that first day, night, day, then night, day...

I wanted to quit the dope though. I knew it was wrong. Each time I got high, I would need more and more to produce a similar effect. The more coke I put in my nose, the faster the dopamine release, the higher the adrenaline rush, ultimately making it almost impossible to go to sleep. You combine sleep deprivation with larger quantities of drug use, and the influx of dopamine trying to be released that your body can no longer create fast enough from the cocaine charge, and walla, instant negative side effects. All the loss of inhibitions, the solving of world problems, the talking and the pupil dilation becomes paranoia. Uh oh, people see how huge my eyes are. They know I'm high. People see how much I'm talking. They know I'm high. People see how much my nose runs and my body sweats. Even today my sister-in-law notices that I don't sniffle as much as I used too, and she had no idea. Nonetheless my brain tells me everyone knows I'm high. People keep looking at me. Don't look at them Mark. Sneak a peek to make sure though. Uh oh, I think we may have a problem developing, paranoia. Oh, and remember the orgasm feeling it produces in your body? Well, lets just say that your mind opens a door in sexual perversion that you can no longer close. You want to watch pornographic films. You fantasize of women doing disgusting sexual things. You go to the bars to find these women that will let you sexually violate them. You're no longer the same person. It's disgusting!

I kept telling myself this is the last time, the last weekend, the last month. Then I turned 26. Then it was October, then November, and then December. I wanted a way out. Make it stop. I didn't know how. The drugs owned me. The lifestyle owned me. I finally wrecked my car in January of 1999. I blacked out leaving a nightclub in Tacoma, Washington and plowed my car into someone's house. I remember staring at the car as it was wedged on the lawn and piled in the front porch. That was my fifth and final car wreck. I was arrested with a .147 blood alcohol content. The scary thing is that the night of my accident, I knew I was going to do something. It was as if I didn't have it in me to ask for help and I needed to create a bad decision, drama. Chaos to get out. That's how my mind worked. A worse situation to leave the one I was in.

I got what I wanted. Relief from the chaos and parental help. I filed for a deferred prosecution for the drunk driving charge, and went through the court motions again. Two years of outpatient chemical dependency treatment. It provided some structure in my world. Some structure that if I violated would send me to jail. I think I needed that at the time. I moved back home to pay bills and get back on my feet. I tried being a success at work to get my mind off of the fact that rather than finally almost being off of probation for all of my past crimes, I just added five years for my drunk driving offense. Great timing too. Effective January 1999 the legislature changed the probationary period of a deferred prosecution from two years to five years. And yes, I knew this law before the accident happened.

So the month of January is starting to become a memorable month for me. When I was three years old, I am rescued from and orphanage in Korea and adopted by an American family. My adoption birthday is January 17. When I was 22, I get released from Thurston County jail after a long, and I mean long tour of incarceration that started three states ago and included five jails and extradition. In January 1996, I trade in my jeans and pretend to leave my criminal past behind as a bad memory. I re-enroll in college to start a career as a white collar professional. In January 1999, I total my fifth car. What is wrong with January? What is wrong with me?

While at home with my parents trying to keep my self-destructive personal life out of site and out of mind, I take the next year and a half and become the over-achiever, super auditor at work. I was leading audits for the City of Lacey, City of Aberdeen and Hoquiam, Pacific County, Chinook and Illwaco Ports, and many of the school districts. By the winter of 1998, I was promoted as an assistant state auditor III. Which is a lead auditor and the final non-competitive position within the office. In reality this is the last automatic promotion based on longevity rather than professional accomplishments, assuming you're not a complete moron. However, I needed to think it was based on my accomplishments as my motivational factor. I needed to think I was being rewarded for being a diligent employee. I needed to think I was being promoted for more than just showing up to my cubicles on time for the past three years.

After about a year and a half of outpatient substance abuse treatment, I felt I had regained stability in my personal life. Treatment classes were down to once a week, my two weekly 12-step recovery meeting slips were forged, my bills were almost paid again that I incurred from the attorney, court fines, and the many credit cards I maxed during the six-month cocaine and booze bender in Tacoma, Washington. I had a good foundation to start my life over again. I have to ask myself at what point did I decide that manageable debt was my only requirement for foundation building to move out? Nonetheless I was leaving my parent's home, again. I rented a room from Jay, my old college buddy that had moved originally from California. He had just bought a house and his wife was moving out. Okay, they were headed for divorce. He had also just graduated from law school so I thought I was making progress with better friends. Finally some other white-collar professionals to associate with. The reality is that he drank like I did and this put my guilt about my drinking at ease. I no longer felt so bad.

It's the fall of 1999. I'm living back in Tacoma, Washington and for the most part keeping my drinking in check. I felt in enough control of my life because I had managed to not drink before my weekly outpatient classes. Abstinence? Well, I was abstaining from cocaine, isn't that good enough? I felt okay. To help keep myself in check, I developed some new hobbies. One was entertaining myself at the local casinos. My neighbor, who is a 6' foot 8" former basketball player, and I set out to win big. The concept. Everyone is dealt two cards face up, except the blackjack dealer; only their top card is seen. There are a number of face cards that equal 10, aces that are eleven or one, and than the number value of the cards from two through nine. Each person on the table is dealt two cards. If you get two that match in value, you can split them and receive one more card on each of them, essentially creating two hands from the one set of cards you were originally dealt. Each person is asked it they like their hand of cards, or if they would like to be dealt another card. For example, if you have a four and a face card, you're hoping to get the dealer to give you a seven or less from the next card on the in the deck. As long as you don't go over 21, which is considered a bust and you forfeit your money you've bet, then you're still in the game. If you're okay with your hand, you waive off adding anymore cards to your hand, and wait for the dealer to flip their bottom card over. You're hoping that the combination of your cards is closer to 21 than the blackjack dealer, thus allowing you to win the amount of your bet. The easy way to win is if the blackjack dealer gets 22 or more, than everyone that is still left on the table automatically wins the amount of their wager. And the bonus, if you have an ace and a face card, you have an instant blackjack. You receive your wager and a half. Seems easy enough. The odds are definitely in my favor. Why? I don't know but they must be.

After several months of playing cards at the casino, I'm totally in debt, every credit card maxed again, and surviving on payday loans. Oh, pay day loans. You'll like this one. If you borrow $500 for two weeks against your future payroll check, it will only cost you a mere $75 to buy your postdated check back. Multiply that by four institutions and I'm paying $600 a month in loan fees. I sold my $4,500 home stereo and was buying gas with $.50 cent pieces from the casinos. That's what they give you when you get a blackjack. Things were still manageable though. Not by the standards of others, but manageable in my head.

Back to the cards. I figured out what I was doing wrong. For starters, the dealer has to take a card for anything less than 17. So if their top card is six, most people stay on their hand hoping the dealer's bottom card is a face card, and they receive one more to bust. If you don't know the rules and say have a total of 13, you hit and take the 10 and bust, the entire table gets pretty upset with you for taking what would have been the dealer's next card. You're real popular if you end up taking the dealer's bust card allowing the house, which is the casino, to win. Another thing I learned is that you don't split every set of cards that match. Two fives equal ten when together. If split and you receive two face cards, each hand is now worth 15, which would have been 20, if I had stayed put and asked for only one card. I was told you only split aces and 8's from some very grumpy people. Rude!

Another thing is that I was not betting enough money on each hand. You can go all night playing the same wager. Win some, lose some, but you never really get ahead of the game. So I raised the wager occasionally from $5 bets to $25. That way I would receive a higher payout from the wins that are really far and few between. Now it's a timing game. Lose the small hands and win the big ones. You just don't know when they are. Well, I thought I was closer to knowing. There are only a certain number of cards. 33% of the deck is worth 10. It's no longer how close can I get to 21, but how many times the table can work together and watch the dealer bust. I was starting to win money. Lots of money. It wasn't too far out of the ordinary to be in the black two or three hundred dollars. Another problem surfaced though. Walking away. I could have left a winner, but I couldn't walk away. I wanted more money. Towards the later stages of my gambling addiction I was playing on the reservations that allowed $500 per hand. Imagine the amounts when you're playing two or three spots? This allows you to increase your wagers to a thousand dollars a hand. And if you play all seven spots on a table. You get the idea. A two and three thousand dollar swing in one hand was not a big deal anymore. The ultimate lesson in self-control is walking away.

Around December of 2000 my outpatient classes were down to once a month. I had a lot more freedom to, well, to party of course. I needed to make up for lost time. The "good habit" I developed at the casino to stay off the booze was really expensive. I'm convinced I'd rather just drink again. So I'm off to Las Vegas for New years on the strip. I love this town. Non-stop partying. My roommate Jay and I fly down. We stay with his sister and party for a week straight with his niece. I love it. We play rounds of over-priced golf, we hit Studio 54, Coyote Ugly, the Belagio, and the MGM. We gamble and make money, we gamble and lose money, but I don't care. I try sushi for the first time. I'm hooked, I love it. We party like rock stars and put his sisters Christmas reindeer that are all lit up with moving parts, in funny sexual positions for the neighborhood to see. We laugh our selves into drunken sleep every night. Maybe a total of 16-hrs of sleep for the entire five-day trip. But this is my life.

One of our excursions to Las Vegas we fly down and stay at a hotel off the strip. We have a few people fly up to party with us. I get propositioned by a call girl at the blackjack table. She says she's an investment analyst and I should call her for a consultation while I'm in Vegas. She gives me her business card. Nice. Short black cocktail dress, pulled back dark hair and high heels. I don't call her. Only in Vegas, I laugh to myself. Another table two guys tell me they have a comp room. They want me to spend some time in it with them. Thanks, but no thanks. They keep following me. Later, we go up to the room and call escort services. Within 30-minutes we have six different call girls parade our room. They tell us the cost and what they'll do. We settle with one that agrees to stay for a while with all of us. Just another day in Vegas.

In the summer of 1999, I had interviewed and was in the process of being promoted as an assistant audit manager within our technical services division. Also referred as TS. But I received a phone call from the Assistant Director, who said the office had decided to not promote me and they were going to re-open the job. She encouraged me to get more field audit experience before I re-applied. What I heard was that I am not on their A-list of people to be promoted. What I was wondering and felt was, how much of my personal life did they know? Actually, they should have known all of it since my initial application and interview. They knew they were giving me a second chance in life, so I was a little curious of what they were seeing that was not what they had expected from my work performance. I didn't put too much consideration that the effects of the personal decisions of my life could be adversely affecting my professional career at this point.

Nonetheless, one of the women I helped hire and train on Team Olympia was eventually hired into team TS into a vacant assistant audit manager position that was similar to the position I had interviewed for. She had less professional experience than I did. I did nothing about the office's decision, rather; I looked for a way out of Olympia to not become disgruntled with what I perceived as the office politics. In the fall of 1999 I transferred from Team Olympia to Team Tacoma. During this time I began working as the auditor in charge of the state's second largest county, as well as led audits of both housing authorities.

So at this point I feel comfortable with my professional standings and recent advancements. However, I still have a little thing on the back of my mind that is telling me that I cannot let loose and take this world by storm. I can't be Mr. Successful. I still have something that makes me Mr. Self-destruct instead. I'm still on probation for my deferred prosecution for my drunk driving charge. I'm convinced that my monthly outpatient appointments are getting in the way of my lifestyle, both professional and personal. It's holding me back. The legal chains that keep me bound. Was I ready for freedom yet? It's not as if they demanded very much. You had to literally be drunk at the monthly monitoring class to be asked to leave a urine sample that they could check for drugs in your system. After our monthly hour and a half meeting, a group of us would gather in the parking lot up the street and sign each others weekly 12-step recovery program slips for the entire month. I know you would not agree but at this point it would not shock you to know that I completed the outpatient successfully in February 2001. In fact the discharge summary said that, "Mark is an example that deferred prosecution works". The statement in itself is quite significant. The recidivism rate is 99%. I've just joined ranks of the ultra minority. Now I only have three years of unsupervised probation to complete without getting pulled over for another drinking violation, and I'm done with my legal obligations. All of them for the first time since 1991. Of course I never entertained that I wouldn't drink like the program was designed to do, I just committed to not get pulled over by a police officer when I left a bar.

During the course of the next nine months, while working as a lead auditor on Team Tacoma, I had applied for and was not selected for an assistant audit manager position that would have had responsibilities over one of the states larger school districts and some other smaller entities. In the fall of 2000, I was finally promoted to the assistant audit manager position that had responsibilities over the county and housing authorities I was already pseudo-managing, as well as a handful of small towns and schools. After four years, I had finally been promoted into a supervisory capacity. A real promotion, not the non-competitive positions I had gained up until this point. There is a reality breaker though. Because of the turnover in our office, the average length of employment was only 18-months around the State. I could take off the blinders and accept the real fact that a large number of people with less work experience than myself within our office had already been promoted, interviewed, and vacated their positions for new jobs. Really, the office was running out of legitimate prospects. Maybe I earned my promotion, maybe I was the only one left. My looming question of the ages.

In October of 2000, I move from Jay's house. I had to. Although I was recently promoted, I was broke. I couldn't keep up financially with my lifestyle. Las Vegas, gambling, drinking, need I say more? I moved in with an old friend of mine named Jack. I negotiated rent with him. I couldn't afford a measly $400, let alone my other bills that were all in collection status from my gambling. Yeah, to recap I didn't make my millions. We decide that we should grow pot and sell cocaine to get out of debt and create a savings account. Perhaps a head start in society? Jack had a nice two-bedroom home with a huge, windowless basement. We could probably net 12-pounds every eight weeks. That's $36,000 split between two people. He also had an inside connection from this guy in that moved up from Houston, Texas. He could get kilograms of cocaine for around $10,000. Street value for a kilogram is roughly $17,000, if sold in a bulk. However, this hardly pays for the trip to and from Houston for two people, unless you're purchasing three or four kilos at a time. For financially strapped, wanna be drug dealers like us, the real money is breaking one kilogram down and selling by the ounce to the street pushers. There are 2.2 pounds in a kilogram, and 16 ounces in a pound, roughly making 35 ounces that sell for about $600 on the streets. The math looks a little better now. That's $21,000. Of course the big dollars for a small time street pusher is breaking down the ounce and selling small bags to your daily customers. For example, an ounce has 28 grams that sell for $40 a piece. The street pusher nets $520 per ounce. Multiply that by seven days a week.

Fucking moron Mark! For starters, I didn't know enough people to sell that kind of coke too. Secondly, do you realize what happens if you have been fronted a half a kilogram to start your drug business with? You try the product. You don't try snorting little lines from a small baggy that I was used to buying. You take a small spoon, chip off a rock of cocaine from the block, squish it into a nice powdery pile, and snort the whole fucking thing through a rolled up dollar bill. I can't describe this feeling. You go from alive, to god status, to dead in less then ten minutes. Remember the chemical induced paranoia that helped me quit earlier in my life?

Hang on for my next journey. First thing I had to take some time off from work. Hmmm, maybe, 30-days will do. Next, I have to get high. I have to get so fucking high I want to see the walls move. I want to see shadows play hide and go seek. I want to hear voices in my head telling me the cops are coming for me. I want to talk to these voices to play this game of mental psychosis convince them, well, me, that it's all in my head. Mark, get so high so you start hearing things.

So high so you start seeing things. So high that you start getting scared of what lurks around each corner, so high that you're scared at what hides within your own mind.

One night Jack and I were getting high on coke sitting on the couch in his living room. Lights dim, smoking cigarettes, drinking beer, and talking about going to the bar to find some girls to bring back. I can't though. I'm too twacked, I can't leave the house. I can barely get off the couch to snort another line in fear that people are spying on me from the windows, the closets, the stairwells, behind the TV cabinet, under the couch, behind the false wall built in the refrigerator. Really, I can't go in public. Knock, knock, knock. Oh shit, we know it's the cops, who else would it be? We're frozen on the couch, sliding the tray of cocaine on the floor and this girl busts through the front door. She sits in-between us. She takes off her clothes. I don't even know her. She knows the neighbors though. She thought she was at their house. How high is she? How high am I? She didn't stay all night, but regretfully so, she stayed long enough.

At this point everything is a blur. I can't even separate the truth from reality anymore. I go to work when I can and swear the parking garage lady is getting kickbacks. How else do you explain my $30 daily parking tickets? I know the sign says an hour, but does that include me too? Okay, get off the drugs Mark. I get a temporary reprieve. I fly to see my mom and her husband in Arizona, visit Mexico, 5-days to see Sandi and Jay in Maui and I'm back. Completely water logged from all the booze but at least off the sauce, sorry, cocaine for two weeks. Thank God, I can breathe again. No literally breathe again. You have no idea the damage cocaine does to your nasal septum. The only cure is to do more to open the nasal passages. Or you could quit and get long enough for the swelling to go down. Is that really an option?

I fly back into Washington State. This time I'm refreshed and ready to be responsible. Okay, maybe a line of coke, or two, or three, or four, or five… Six months later and I was done. Carrying large quantities of weed in my car, constant traffic of people in and out of the house buying coke, and now Jack and I are talking about going to California to buy pills of ecstasy to sell. Oh my god, what is my life becoming. Am I really a drug dealer? A junkie? Let's not forget my profession that's now hanging by a small thread. Everyone at work is paging me, no one can ever find me. I want to go to work. That's the only safe place for me from the drugs. I just can't get there. I can't stop doing cocaine. I can't even stop looking out the windows staring at people that aren't there, tip toeing around the house in fear that the cops hiding in my walls will hear me, always broke and feeling disgusting inside. Oh, before I forget to mention. The key to making money by selling dope is to actually, sell dope. I snorted mine. And the pot we were going to grow?

In March of 2001 my cocaine abuse is completely out of control. I blame my environment. More importantly, I blame Jack. I know if I can just get out of his home. The place I refer to as the disgusting crack home. Dirty and disgusting. Just bad memory after bad memory after bad memory. So, like always, I run and find a bail out. I move in with my old neighbor. Remember the gambler? For the next four months I stay up late nights doing coke, drinking and still skipping work. Surprise, surprise, problems followed me. Maybe it wasn't Jack's entire fault after all. This stage of my drug use I can't even entertain the notion of doing drugs with someone else, unless I absolutely have too. I'm too wierded out on the chemicals. I wouldn't even want to be around me. I'm using cocaine by myself in complete darkness; tip toeing around in the spare bedroom late at night with the fan on to drown out any noise. Ya know, the noise that comes from sitting on the edge of your bed, crushing a line of cocaine on a CD case, snorting, and hiding the plastic baggy under the bed. Each line intensifies your senses. My stomach could gurgle and I thought I could hear my neighbors telling me to quiet down. I have elevated my drug use to such a pathetic level. My association with my friends is almost non-existent. My daily routine might include 3-days a week of work, local bar for shots of liquor and a baggy of coke for home. I need another break. Another change of scenery because this one sure isn't working.

My annual trip to Maui in October 2001 was a memorable one. I'm sitting with this guy on the airplane who is part owner of one of the golf courses in Maui. He's telling me of his missed financial opportunities in fast food restaurants, land acquisitions, whatever, you name it he's done it. So filthy loaded, rather than changing his diet, he losses weight by flying half way around the world to have a Dr. remove his fat. He's on his return trip from Canada after completing this miracle weight loss program. This time it involved removing some excess, baggy skin as well. His girlfriend picks him up in their two-door explorer. Wow, they've volunteered to give me a ride to the Sheraton in Kaanapali, Maui. Keep in mind I'm traveling to Maui, but I'm flat ass broke. The money I will have to spend I gave too Jay a week ago because I would, as I did, spend everything in my pocket before I met up with him. Really, an airport shuttle or rental car is not in the cards for me. So she whips out a marijuana joint. Okay, I can smoke it. I don't normally smoke pot but hey, I'm in paradise, and they're giving me a ride. Sure, whatever it takes Mark. I get ripped. My heads light, my eyes are blurred, every thing now seems ultra creepy. I look around, I'm stuck in the back seat of their explorer with two people I don't even know getting high in Maui.

Breath Mark, you're just trippin'. Can pot actually make you this paranoid, or is it the residual effect from the sleep deprivation and chemical brain alteration from a year and a half cocaine bender? Maybe even all the booze? Or, maybe the pot is laced with another drug? Maybe it's the pot. Hawaiian pot. Maybe it's a combination of all these things. I don't know, but can you imagine how long this would take me to process all these thoughts? She starts talking about this poor fool that took his car in to get it checked out. He later crashed his car and died in the wreck. They start laughing. Ha, ha. They made it look like an accident but really they cut his brake line. They She keeps looking at me in the rear view mirror. He keeps looking at me from his passenger seat. More pot? No! Now I'm freaked. Holy-shit, they're going to crash this car, kill me and make it look like an accident. I start looking at the side of his face. I'm so high right now. There is a solid line from his forehead down to his chin. Baggy skin, off-centered face, maybe some bad plastic surgery. It now makes sense why he was in Canada. He's a fuckin' mobster in the witness relocation program. They made him lose weight, gave him a new face and here I sit. I'm going to die at the hands of some ungrateful, unreformed mobster. Shit!

My hearts racing so fast. The car seems like they're driving real slow, I'm hyper ventilating trying to keep a straight face, but I can't move, I can't even say a word. All I can do is smoke more of the joint they keep giving me. It's in your head Mark. Why would they want to kill you? Let's see, you make great money at your job, you've partied with a lot of rich people, your dad's the Lieutenant

Governor....Oh shit! He thinks I'm fuckin' rich! Wait, I'm not, most the stories on the plane about business ventures I made up. My mouth won't move though. My heart is going to jump out of my chest. I'm convinced that he's going to make some lame ass excuse to stop at his $2,000,000 mansion that he couldn't stop talking about on the plane, offer to show me around the house. You like the view? Yeah, right on the oceanfront. Nice vaulted ceilings, nice tiled floors, nice spacious rooms, hey, is that a movie room too... slam! Congratulations Mark. You've just been kidnapped. They're going to beat you, dress you in leather, stick a ball in your mouth and make you a sex slave. When they've had enough, they're going to try and ransom you back for money. Please, God. No. Breathe, breathe, you can make it through this Mark. More dope? Fuck no! That's what I wanted to say. No thanks, I'm pretty good. That's what I really said.

He looks at his wife and says, since home is on the way, I've got to stop and pee. Oh God, it's going to happen. Mark, when they stop the car jump out and run. Shit, I can't, I'm in the back seat of a two-door car. That's convenient. Yeah, for them...kidnappers! So I saw the house, they dropped me off at the Sheraton. I even golfed with them the following day. I guess they were messing with me. Or the drugs were messing with me. Maybe I was messing with me. It was kind of a rush though.

After two weeks of blistering sun we were in route back to Seattle, Washington. This time I meet these people on the plane that are play-wright directors in Olympia, Washington. They gave me a part in a play called Karnak and Luxor that opened on the same day as the Iraq war. He was gay and just wanted me to run around in a skirt. I'm not. My character name was Jubade. When it was my turn too read scripts he would say, "I want Ju-Body". Funny, funny. Nonetheless the play was a neat experience. Oh well. Another story, another time.

I'm back in Tacoma and really trying to get my life back together. Where do I start though? Fuck it. Work at this point was almost non-existent. My schedule, my completely tailored schedule, included an early morning meeting at an audit site, office around 11-ish for lunch, afternoon emails, phone calls, delegation of responsibilities too co-workers, off-site afternoon appointment with a constituent or auditee, careful, you can read my timesheet too. In the early afternoon, if I weren't drinking yet, I would grace my co-workers with a token phone call telling them I was leaving my appointment and calling it a day. So that takes care of my boss and co-workers. Phone on do not disturb and screening calls on my cell phone, takes care of bill collectors. My time is finally freed up to enjoy the finer things in life. Every dollar I made went to my three greatest causes, or curses; black jack at the casinos by day and cocaine and booze by night.

This lifestyle can only be managed for so long. You get sloppy, you get tired, and you get too preoccupied. The bases you are covering start becoming uncovered. My boss is pulling me aside about once a month with little hints like; the accounting department is monitoring timesheets, Diane is constantly calling Olympia looking for you, and your not returning voicemails and pages from your pager. Mark, perception, where you at? If people perceive something then it must be. Hmmm? That's a nice thought. Are you kidding me? My life's fine bro. I watch football games from the suite in the Seahawks stadium on the 40 yard line, watch the mariners from the suite between home plate and first base, take three to four vacations a year, I can have any woman I choose, and you're concerned about my perception at work? Seems like you just need to remember you're the tied down, shackled, married one, not me. Thanks for the "concern" though. Maybe I'll get a "non-life" and spend more time at the office, perhaps become as work involved as all the other people that have nothing outside of work. Actually, take away the drugs and that was the thing I was trying to do the whole time. Lucky me though, I would soon get a lesson in respect of others. Real soon.

During my second audit cycle as an assistant audit manager, in late 2001, a new audit manager position was created in Olympia. This one would over see the software conversion for our office, create help desks to field technical questions by auditees and auditors, expand office liaison positions with outside entities, enhance internal office training. I submitted my application. There were only a couple applicants that met the qualifications. After six years with the office and my experience with state audits, local audits, federal audits, financial audits... I was one of them. After the job closed I was informed they were going to re-open the job search. I was also informed that a co-worker was asked to apply from the Olympia office. Nonetheless, I was not interviewed and she was offered the audit manager position. It doesn't stop here though. In 2001, I made the final cut to an Olympia audit manager position that was vacated. Although considered, I was not promoted. They had already recruited someone from the Bellingham office several years earlier to work on the team and groom to take the position. That's how my mind interpreted these decisions. I didn't fathom that my personal life was a factor. How could it be, I have nothing but accolades in my personnel file. Maybe it's complete denial on my part of un-written insight of my personal life by my employer, or, well, lets not go there.

Despite the hiring and promotion practices of the agency I was beginning to see, I tried to maintain a positive attitude and maintain focus on my career. This is the era that I took on a lot of voluntary positions within the office to enhance my marketability. I wanted to be prepared for future promotions. One area specifically was with the housing authorities. There are 42 of them in the State of Washington. I didn't know at the time the amount of work I was to inherit. What I found out was the office was in high-risk status with the Department of Housing and Urban Development (HUD) for audits not meeting qualifications. What I unraveled was a list of former employees that fell victim to their cause of improvement. What I opened was a can of worms that later made me a candidate for the vacant fall guy position, just like the others before me. I don't care though. I like the challenge. I like the dual. Mind versus mind. You're on. I will lose in the end though.

So that was work. Somewhat promising again. However, my personal life was hideous. After about ten months of partying and gambling again, I had lost almost everything, I got even deeper in debt. Yes, you would be surprised at the financial lenders that crawl out of the woodwork chasing people like me. I moved into another friend of mine's house where I negotiated a way to live for cheap rent, again. I was sleeping on the couch and supposed to help him with his books for his engineering business. I never did. Doing drugs and missing work was now just a part of my life. What made him think my commitment to his business would be any different. Why even bother. Stay until they ask me to leave. I had at this point accepted that everyone had internal problems. External success' were just disguises. All people were the same and it was pointless to try and change.

This lasted for two and a half months until I rented an apartment with one of my former Tacoma roommates in Federal Way. Drugs progressed and financially things just got worse, if you can even fathom that. I exploited a bank account of my brothers for thousands of dollars. My family intervened and I moved in with my little sister Sherri and her husband to Seattle. Nothing changed. After four months I moved again. This time back to Jack's house in Tacoma. Yes, the source of all lot of my cocaine. Hang on. I reunited with the cocaine scene very heavily. Well, I never really stopped, but when the use goes from little street baggies back too large quantities. Well, just hold on. I know I am. Holding on to anything for moment of self-sanity. I was about 28 years old at this point. I'm mixing drug use and gambling to levels I never before imagined. My roommate was selling coke for a dealer. This guy was connected in Chicago and Texas. Oh yeah, he was also on parole in Washington. But what it meant for me was virtually free dope. My cocaine use at this point in life is more or less a daily habit. I stopped fighting. Why bother. My point of existence is to gamble and do more drugs. I was no longer gambling at the casinos to win. I was no longer snorting cocaine to play a head game in my mind. I was no longer drinking booze to get a little buzz. I was no longer driving my car to stay on the road. I was trying to kill myself by wrecking everything. Hate life, bottle feelings, numb pain, hate life, bottle feelings, numb pain, hate…

After about seven months of this I rented a room from my former gambling buddy, again. The drugs and gambling continued and I couldn't even pay rent let alone my bills. Let me rephrase this. I stopped paying rent and bills. I didn't care. This lasted about three months and I moved back into Jay's home. I stayed there this time for about a year and half. Nothing changed.

X

Drugs, Alcohol and Gambling; The Final Blow

February 2002 I start my evening with my roommate at a sports bar around 6pm. Three drinks later we're on the road to a small, whole in the wall lounge, the infamous place where I was Billy Idol for a night. Costumes, Karoake, oh well, another story for another time. We meet up with a couple friends who are celebrating his new job. One of them has been recently signed as the back-up pitcher for a professional baseball team. Congratulations. Let's do shots of Tequila. I'm buying, we're all drinking and you better make your 6am flight. The other, a city cop that I later moved in with his ex-wife. Does my lifestyle ever end?

My roommates blitzed, I should have been, but the last couple shots I was spitting them back in the beer bottle pretending to drink my chaser. Smart man! Whatever. So I leave the restaurant and lo and behold, I pull out in front of a State Trooper. Yep, my dad's employees. Well, kind of anyway. Party lights. The reason we pulled you over, and I emphasize we, it was trooper-training night and they were going to do a routine stop until they smelled the booze. The car gets impounded, I blow a .097 blood alcohol content, and they let me go home. Good, didn't have to use the all mighty "dad" card. More drinking, more cocaine, more gambling, less work, less bills, more coke, more booze, more grandiose money making plans, does it ever end? No, in the tail end of May or early June 2002, I receive the dreaded when I open my mail. Congratulations, we've decided to charge you with drunk driving. A DUI? Are you kidding me! I cannot believe they waited four months. Maybe I should have used the all mighty dad card that evening. Would it have helped though? Maybe even made it worse. Yeah, they charge me sooner? I'm pissed. I'm really pissed off. Time for an attorney. I can't get another DUI, I haven't even completed the five year deferral for the first one. One attorney, two attorney, three attorney, four. Oh, that was the magic number. Four attorneys on this one. Nonetheless, out of sight out of mind.

So this actually slows me down. I dive back into work a little bit. By this point I'm kind of the roller coaster employee. I'm up, on fire, good, good, good, then vroooom, I take the down turn, the loop, the hard corners, and then crawl back up. One of my audits has a problem with its contract to one of the smaller cities. Apparently, the money the cops are giving to the drug informants, the people arrested with drug charges and offered a way out to set up a drug bust on their suppliers, is not making back into the evidence room when the arrest is made. What? It's actually easier than you would think. You give the informant $500 to buy some dope, make the arrest when the suspect gets out of the car; confiscate all the dope and cash. Let's see, $100 to evidence and a small bag of weed. Pocket the rest. That's what I thought the sheriff department informant was telling me.

Dangerous for me. I was so high on coke all the time, I stepped way back on my supervisory role. I avoid most of the meetings with the informants, the sheriffs, internal affairs, Council members, really just organizing and reviewing workpapers. I was actually a little afraid of the cops seeing me dope sick all the time. But a little intrigued at the same time. We look at the detective accounting ledgers and bank accounts in question. One of them we find over $60,000 in unaccounted for deposits. Wow, and this was only one cop. What about the other accounts? The squeal. We question more cops. They feel the pressure. One tells us; if you think this is bad, check out the federal agency of the task force. An internal auditor says, whoagh, we don't touch that. I get a call. I can't, sorry, I won't tell you who it was, and what the conversation was. But I will tell you I was officially done chasing cops.

Long story short we work with about three internal affairs and five criminal investigators for about six months. Three cops get referred for prosecution, 90-officers lose their job when the city terminates its $12 million dollar a year contract with the Sheriff's Office. The reality is that most of the cops were legitimately up-holding the law. A large percentage of them were re-hired by the City when it constructed its own police force. My job as an auditor unfortunately was only exposed to mishandlings of government.

So work frustrates me, my private life frustrates me. I find self-fulfillment in nothing. I drink to lose reality, and my lost reality forces me to drink. In August of 2002, I meet Marisa at the bar. She's hot. Everyone's drooling. I take her home. She's 23, thin and a party girl. I get her pregnant. But in a sick way I'm happy inside. I want something to change. This became my new reason for living. People at work were happy for me, at least the few I told, the cocaine was really being cut down from my life, I was now thinking of ways to move her in and raise a family. I was in love. Wait, I don't even know her. I'm not in love. I want to be with her but I don't. I can't stop sleeping with other women. Sometimes with more than one involved. Yet it's my own secret. I never tell anyone who I sleep with, not even my friends.

In November of 2002, she informs me she had a miscarriage. Whatever, I'm done then, back to the coke. In actuality I was pretty hurt inside. I can't fathom having a little me running around. Maybe a little me that provides the closure to the little me that I am too somebody else that abandoned me so long ago. I just didn't know how to process any of these feelings. Good ones, bad ones, blah ones. Every feeling and emotion never made it past my guards. They were never pulled up to have to be pushed down. They were already suppressed. This just the reinforcement of pain. I was the walking dead. I become angry and blame. She's the party girl that lost my child. It's her fault. And my neighbor, my old gambling buddy, you're having sex with her friend so you won't even tell me the truth. The truth that I later found out that she had an abortion that you knew the whole time and lied to my face about. Coke will cure that pain though. And so will booze and gambling, that my neighbor will now pay the tab because he doesn't know that I know he knows. I'm sick!

I went through what I thought at the time was a miscarriage that hardly phased me emotionally, because at this point I had suppressed any feelings of life in me at all. I don't even know how to feel anything anymore let alone grieve. My pending DUI was reduced to a reckless driving, which revoked my deferred prosecution for my DUI in 1999. This was a real treat. Besides the few hours I spent in jail for my first DUI, I hadn't been incarcerated since 1993. Now because the revocation of my deferred prosecution, I have to turn myself into jail for a night. I hate myself! I hate my life! I hate my decisions! I hate my friends! I hate my drugs! I hate my booze! I hate my gambling! I hate my job! Nonetheless, I was still excelling at work. I know the dark pages paints a character that is not fully vindicated. The reality is that I'm actually pretty smart, an excellent support and trainer for the office employees, and able to balance a large workload despite my unreliability. This baffled everyone. Some just assumed I was always in meetings, so busy and working weekends, my token façade. It pays to be seen, even if for only ten minutes. Others knew I was slacker and it was their mission to catch me. Nonetheless, my completion of job duties spoke for themselves. My projects were always on time. My public relations with auditees were impeccable. And my billing responsibilities of audits were 1/3 of the entire team.

I created a consulting firm to keep my mind of off Marisa, my lost child, my abandonment, my life of frustrations, my life of inadequacy, my broken life. I excel at this too. During my nights and weekends, I sign a contract as an investment consultant for the State's largest house banked casino. This made my material world even worse. Now, I was meeting people with lots of money. I had access to their sporting event suites, private clubs, and phat weekend excursions. The hardest part of all this lifestyle was the reward of more money. The translation for me was more money, more booze, more drugs, more gambling and more binge drinking vacations. I was so out of touch with reality. I would sit in a lounge feeling untouchable. Then rendezvous with my drug dealer in a sleaze bar. How much does a small piece of self-sanity cost?

In July of 2003, I was sentenced to 15-days of electronic home monitoring for my reckless driving stemming from February 2002. Good, that's manageable, all I have to do is take a two-week vacation, stay at home with an ankle bracelet, don't drink and don't get high.

This is my answer. My drugs keep me from solidifying any money contracts in my consulting firm. My drugs keep me from over coming my hurdle of promotion at work. This is my way out. The much-needed time I've been looking for to get off the drugs for good. And wow, I have till the end of August to complete the 15-days. Thank you your honor. You have no idea. So August comes up and then passes by, still can't stop getting high long enough to pass a mandatory urine analysis for electronic home monitoring. Can't I pull four days of sobriety together? I'm so pissed off at myself. Four fuckin' days of sobriety, pass my piss test, sleep for two weeks and I'm done. By, by reckless driving. By, by court. By, by legal system forever.

In September I received a warrant in the mail. Dear Mr. Owen, your license has been suspended and a warrant issued for your arrest for failure to comply. Great, now I don't even have a license. Sure hope I don't get pulled over driving to audit sites. That would be a real treat. I can see the headlines now. Auditor is taken into custody by local police for a warrant that was revealed when he was pulled over for failing to have a clean windshield, or some stupid bullshit like that. By the way, my car has no insurance or tabs, in case I forgot to mention that earlier? So I really don't want to get pulled over. I really don't even want to schedule audit meetings with any law enforcement agencies in fear they'll recognize my face as a wanted fugitive. Ya know, because my reckless driving warrant takes precedence over, say a rapist or murderer. My head is so twacked right now. What's wrong with me? And I'm so negative. I smile but inside I'm so negative. Where is reality? Or is this my reality? Forever?

Nonetheless I try. I take on another project at work. Another project that is well above and beyond my job description. I call it, one last attempt to enhance my marketability, too get the attention of my boss. If he doesn't notice now and promote me, well fuck him then, that's what my attitude was. This project included a nine-month accounting service project for a small city. I disclosed almost $900,000 in un-collected Local Improvement District funds, in the first two years of the special assessed tax. This is not good. This has been our audit for several years. This makes the office look really bad. I need to wash my hands of this project. I know it, the City knows, even my bosses in Olympia know it. There is nothing more powerful then the closed-door meetings they had. Thank God though; I'm out of it. Any Reporting???

In the later parts of 2003, I had interviewed for the Team Lynnwood audit manager position. I made the final round, or top three, and on paper was qualified. I had two years of state audit experience, five years of local audit experience, assistant audit manager to the state's second largest county and the housing authority liaison for the entire state of Washington effectively making this position, all though an increase in compensation, a reduction of responsibilities and title. The person promoted was less qualified than me and hand selected. This event in my head was translated into race discrimination. I can't even fathom anything otherwise. Look at my personnel file! Or is it my personal life?

In late 2003 I had also interviewed for the Team Higher Education audit manager position. This was a team that had collapsed and was combined with Team King County and Seattle for a couple years. I made the final round and on paper was again qualified for the position. You can't even compare us on paper. I'm so disgusted with my employer now. How do you keep promoting people with five years less experience than me? Does not my nine years count for anything? So once again I translate this to race discrimination. This time I do some research within the office. I'm surprised to find out that during the past couple years, two of the three minority audit managers left the agency. I don't know why. I have my suspicions though. Even worse, I am one of a very, very, small handful of minority assistant audit managers within the State. Keep looking. Hmmm, there are only a few minorities within the entire agency? This doesn't add up for me. I have to face the reality that I may be a victim of race discrimination. Or, could my boss see that my personal life was affecting my job? The unmanageability of my personal life that was creeping into my professional life would tie my hands from ever asking the million-dollar question, even though I felt I knew the answer already. If this were chess, check mate. You win! Maybe, I'm not so smart after all. If it were my personal life affecting my professional career, a corrective action plan would be warranted with a temporary job reclassification, so I could get some help. Your internal policy, not mine, please use it. If it's race, there's nothing I can do. You win. I'm to scathed to ever make that case. I felt at the time I knew what the answer is.

Now it's late fall and my roommate is making wedding plans with his soon to be wife. After being roommates for the past three years, and literally having daily contact over brews for the past seven years, he was leaving for marriage. New wife, new home, new boat, new dog. I was jealous. In fact angry inside and I didn't even know it. Despite the fact that I had a great career of over nine years, a luxury vehicle, frequent vacationer to Maui and Las Vegas, newly budding consulting firm, and a contract to buy his old house, his leaving provided me a perfect reason to self-destruct. I was feeling abandoned and rejected by another human. I was feeling lost and alone and un-able to take care or protect myself from harms way. History repeating itself from when I was two and a half years old all over again. All these emotions and I didn't even know that I was feeling these feelings inside. Why? I was never sober long enough to feel.

Ultimate destruction phase enter stage left. My boss and I pulled into the parking garage , after having lunch, and my car was no longer in its parking stall. No! It had my paycheck in it that I hadn't even cashed yet. Okay, breathe, call the bank. Sure enough, it was finally repossessed. Holy shit! My car was just re-possessed. How am I going to get to work? Stay calm. I made a wild deal with one of my co-workers. I'll give you half the money now and the other half in a month for you car. She took it. I was back on the road that evening driving a pretty nice little Honda Accord. Okay, all is not lost. Off to the bar! Work, cocaine, booze, gambling, dodge bill collectors, less work, more cocaine, more booze, more gambling, dodge bill collectors... So the cycle repeats itself day in and day out. I'm bored, but stuck. I want something to change, but what? How? Why? Somehow, I manage to squeeze in a couple hours to get some free food and gifts during Thanksgiving and Christmas at my parent's house. I barely leave the driveway, and I'm already on the phone to my drug dealer, as my car is headed up I-5 back to Tacoma, Washington. I can't miss a beat. I've got to get high.

My last trip to Maui was for my roommate's wedding in February of 2004. I now had to face the reality of my financial codependency relationship with him ending. I knew things would collapse soon because I would have to rely on myself. This was the icing on the cake. I couldn't get myself to even show up too work anymore. Almost all of my paid leave is exhausted at this point. All I did in life now is party and gamble at the casinos. I know lived with the fact that my compulsions were so out of control, that I was looking for a way to end it all. My recap of what I wanted an end too; From the time of October 2003 to April 2004, I had lost two cars, paperwork for my home purchase fell through, I gambled and drugged away about $50,000 more dollars. My bar tabs were about $2,000 a month, $2,000 to $3,000 a month for gambling and $1,000 for cocaine. The all night cocaine benders had me on the edge of death and sanity. The losses at the casinos drove the hammer of self-misery and my job kept my hope of any self worth alive. After Maui, I was faced with the fact that I was about to become homeless. I move in with Kayla and her two kids. However, I spend most of my nights in hotel rooms doing dope. I paid her rent though. This was the first time I actually paid on time. Maybe I would transform from the ultra shitty roommate to Mr. Responsible? Maybe her and her kids would provide me that motivation. Probably not. Look at me. I'm not worth it!

XI

Final Blow For Real This Time

As if the negative feelings from the office were not enough, my chemical dependency problem, I was dealing with, was growing exponentially. I trudged along. Trudged along to the point that it finally consumed me. It affected the performance of my work and my ability to think logically and make rational decisions. I had George following my whereabouts from Olympia, Washington. I also feel these performance issues affected the decision to not promote me into a management position at work. Like upper management was concerned, but not too the point of making or presenting a corrective action plan to help me. Therefore, I self destructed, in my disease of alcoholism ultimately losing my job, my career, my profession, while my employer sat back and watched it all happen. No negative entries on my personnel file that keeps them in a position of, gee, I don't know what happened to Mark. He just left. Nine and a half year career! Too bad. I needed help. I needed counseling and placement into another area of the office until I could get healthy. Both options the employer had scripted in policy, but for whatever reason didn't offer me.

They let my disease overcome me and watched me fail. Fail to the point that my payroll check was lost in the mail and not received by me. I filed an affidavit for a lost payroll warrant. Later the other check arrived and I cashed it as well. The problem is that I was so chemically affected, and my financial status was such a mess at this point, my head was not clear enough to differentiate or know whether this was not my regular payroll warrant I was receiving in the mail. Rather, what I had opened and cashed was the lost payroll check that I had already received a replacement too. After being confronted by the fiscal manager, I immediately made arrangements to re-pay my oversight. I went back home and looked at the payroll envelope. Portland, Oregon! Now I know the reason it was lost. It was post-marked and sent to Portland, Oregon. Why? I felt like I was being set up by my employer. My chemically affected brain was so altered at this point the only thing I was the fact that I needed help. I needed a way out. I needed some peacefulness back into my life. I needed off death's roller coaster that owned me.

Nonetheless, the elected state auditor and his Chief of Staff, met with me at a local coffee shop. I explained what happened with the payroll check. I also explained my years of chemical dependency and gambling addiction. I asked for help. They told me about someone close to them that he knew that went through chemical dependency treatment at Sundown M Ranch. He finished the conversation by telling me to take control of this bad situation. I respect those words from him. However, the reality is that he never offered me help through the state's employee assistance program, or placed me on administrative leave, or developed a corrective action plan to reassign me within the office as they sort out this situation, like their internal policy allows. Rather, he said, "I can't have you auditing like this." You can either be fired, or resign. My chemical affected brain could not process this decision. I wanted to wait until my father returned from Spain. I wanted an attorney. I felt under pressure to make a decision in that room. I forcefully resigned from a nine-year profession in that coffee shop.

I felt betrayed by my employer. People suffering from this should not fall victim to the mistreatment that I received. Especially when it's escalated to the point it's affecting my work. My employer knows more about my personal decisions than they will ever be willing to say, as they watched my life fall apart, and that's the unfortunate bottom line. People should be able to ask for help and use the resources they have, and if offered from their employer, too get healthy and not lose their job and financial well being for their family.

My parents returned from Spain a couple days later and they contacted Sundown M Ranch. In the mean time I exposed my gambling and drug problems with all my friends and co-workers. Although the human resource manager informed everyone they were not allowed to talk about what I said in or out of work, this bad situation now ended up being the first time in my life that I gave up and asked for real help. People helped me. Jay's new wife gave me self-help books and made me stay at their house; I filed for bankruptcy, contacted my attorney for my reckless driving warrant and I was headed for chemical dependency treatment. Wait. Was there a pit stop ahead? With all my good intentions, after a week of being free of drugs, alcohol and gambling, I went on a four-day cocaine and alcohol bender. It started on Thursday April 29th. I arrived in Tukwila at the casinos corporate office for one of my consulting contracts. I printed flyers and marketing aids for my business, since that was my only source of income now, rounded up casino chips, cards, prizes and black jack dealers for what would later prove to be the final alcohol party I would throw, completed my intake interview with Sundown M Ranch and was scheduled for treatment on May 3, 2004.

Evening rolled around, I drove home which was only about the third time I saw my roommate, her two kids and the house I was paying rent in for the past two months. Between my shoes, suit and watch I was clothed with about $2,000 in what I called arrogance armor to keep the poor and un-connected away from me. That way only the shakers and movers would even dare approach my domain. Like always, I arrived fashionably late. This time too my own party. Lucky for me, my old roommate took it upon himself to set up the card tables and chips. But all that just kept my ideals going that the world revolved around me and you were here to take care and clean up after me. At my former job the email was set-up with last name then first. So in a search I would never appear and people would have to remember to type in my first name to send me an email. I used to tell people it's easier for them to change then me. The sad part is that I truly believed that at the time.

I make my grand entrance to the private club where about 20 people are already gathered together drinking and socializing. The club spans the 16th floor of the largest building in downtown Tacoma, Washington. The restaurant and bar over look the bridges, downtown port and the Puget Sound. I was hosting a casino night social party for about 85 club-members. We brought in four black jack tables, dealers and prizes for the winners. We had hors d'oeuvres and all the booze you could drink. At this point it had been 10 days since my last inhale of a cigarette, liquefied drop of booze, snort of powdered cocaine, and loss of control on a black jack table. I was starting to feel pretty good. Uh oh, maybe even good enough to have a beer with my "friends". My best friend didn't think so. No way. He drank nonalcoholic beer with me all night so that I wouldn't look beerless or feel powerless to the other members. He stuck by my side.

Around 10:30pm after my closer friends left I quit fighting. I drank probably six straight shots of scotch. Normally you sip, not me, I had some time to make-up. I chased those with 3-4 bud lights. I was hardly fazed. I outlasted all the partygoers. Even the die-hards I used to close the place down with during the week. My mission was complete. My last run before treatment was just starting. I didn't stop it. I chose it. I wanted it. It was time to lose. Time to forget all those that cared. Time to forget that I lost my career of ten years. Time to forget I filed for bankruptcy. Time to forget I lost two cars. Time to forget I gambled away what could have been the down payment for the home I was living in. Time to forget my new roommate and her two beautiful kids that I absolutely adored. Time to forget the child I lost. Time to forget the pain I feel inside everyday. Time to lose and let go.

Around midnight I headed for the bar. Had shots of henesy, again, a sipping drink for everyone but me, and met my drug dealer for a couple grams of coke. I had the garage code to the old place that was owned by my former roommate that was empty and being painted. I drove to that house drunk and high. Parked in the garage with all the lights off, and held a bag of dope sniffing my feelings away. The next morning around 11am, I connected with another dealer that only lived a few miles away for another couple grams. Snuck back to the house and snorted those in a few short hours. No booze though. I was too high to drive to the store. I was too high to be in my own skin. I was chemically scitzed and physically captive to the thoughts in my head.

I finally came down long enough to get a couple hours of sleep. I headed out in the early evening to another bar on pacific avenue, to meet another dealer and pick up a teenier of very good coke this time. Good meaning it wasn't cut with all the under-the-kitchen-counter shit the other stuff was. This dealer was an old hippy guy that didn't step on his stuff, the term for keeping your drugs clean. It cost more, but the high was so much cleaner and lasted so much longer. I drank beers with him, did shots, played pool and snorted lines off the back corner table of the bar. My sinuses, ears, nose and throat were so trashed. The first 10 seconds of every line made my eyes water in pain until my body from the shoulders up became numb and legs and arms turned to jello. This lasted until 10pm or so. I broke down and called a buddy of mine watching the empty casino being built on 6th avenue. Got dope, got beer, I'm on my way. The saddest thing is I hated his company when doing drugs and that's all we did together. Fed each other's misery. He'd get high, play video games, never say a word; cough, sweat and he stunk all the time. Of course so did I. But I tolerated that because it was better than sitting in an empty house, twacked and completely scared that cops and invisible people were messing with me.

Well, surprise, surprise. He hadn't been calling me because he had dope too. Thanks friend. Call me when you don't have it and hope that I do, then no word when you finally have your own. Who cares though? I didn't have to get high by myself for one night. And to top it off, he had two grams, almost an eight ball of cocaine between the two of us to split. The next evening, which was now Saturday May 1, 2004, we rolled to the bar on South Tacoma way around 11pm to pick up two more grams of coke. I was physically exhausted, hungry and mentally gone. I couldn't breathe through my nose, snot was constantly draining and every part of my body was covered in sweat and stale cigarette odor. As we parked the car my dad called. Hello? It must have sounded like someone was pinching my nose. He called to make sure I was okay. Sure, things are going great. Still clean and looking forward too treatment. Bullshit! I was sitting in front of the bar excited to get more dope. I'm sorry dad. I never meant to lie and hurt you, I just needed more dope. Something you may never understand. Something I will have to fight to over come.

121

The next morning my buddy went for another dope run at the Indian Casino. Hmmmm... black jack and a baggy of dope, I'll take two. I tried to guzzle warm beers and sleep while he was gone so I would be rested for another round. He came back a couple hours later. Ouch, that first line burns. Made me puke. Made my eyes tear up. The pain starts all over. Oh wait, there it goes. Numbness, lightheaded, blurr, melt, and nothing. No pain, I feel great. But the mental sketches are close behind. We finally left the empty casino around 3pm, went to another friends house. At around 6pm I did my last line of coke, drank my last drink of booze and went home. Not alone though. I had my head and my thoughts. Thoughts of who I was and what I am. What did I just lose?

As the booze and cocaine wear off I sit and reflect to the things I had lost. The big one, my nine years at the Washington State Auditor's Office. I reflect back to January 1996 when I started as an audit intern. In August of 1998 I was promoted to an Assistant State Auditor II (staff auditor). In October of 1999 I promoted as and Assistant State Auditor III (audit lead). In November of 2000 I was promoted as the State's youngest Assistant State Audit Manager. My responsibilities included supervisory of approximately five full time auditors whose combined annual billings were approximately $700,000 and audit responsibility of $800,000,000 in annual operating budgets. My duties included a review of classified documents and public records within all financial accounting systems, software and departments of state and federally funded entities within Pierce County. As a representative of the State Auditors Office I communicated the results of these audits to the governing bodies that included both elected and appointed officials, department directors and CEO's.

In addition to these statutory responsibilities, from 2001 through 2004, I re-established communication with key governmental agencies that was terminated when the State Auditor was elected in the early 1990's. I revamped and was promoted as the liaison for the State Auditors Office to communicate audit policies with the United States Department of Housing and Urban Development, United States Department of Agriculture (rural grants), Association of Washington Housing Authorities and the Washington Housing Accounting and Administrative Professionals. I was responsible for coordinating annual workshops and centralizing communication between these governments, constituents and our office to ensure a central point of contact as well as consistent communication to all parties regarding audit responsibilities and reporting requirements. My most significant accomplishments include being an advisor and liaison for governmental entities, exposing corruption and revamping accounting procedures.

Trying to grasp for anything positive, I try and smile but I realize I've thrown everything away. Why? Because I felt like nobody loved me and wouldn't understand if I expressed that to them? It was time to stop hurting myself and others. It was time to die!

XII

Chemically Induced Schizophrenia

The late stages of my drug use was a journey in mental psychosis. I would do lines of cocaine, sometimes a teenier at a time to see how high I could get. People would tell me of the voicemails I would leave them completely frantic that the cops we're going to break into the house and arrest me. I would run from beings that didn't exist in my room for fear they would catch me. They were trying to possess me. Like a demon they were sexually assaulting me. I would try and cover my mouth, my ears, my nose, my eyes, to not be violated. But there was never anything physically there. Just my drugs and my psychosis. I was too afraid to drink a beer, to afraid to light a cigarette, too afraid to open my eyes. I would visually see shit, urine and seamen being thrown at me, landing on my clothes, inside my water, my booze, my coke would taste like Ajax. I would hide under my covers with my shoes on and fully clothed so if I got arrested I would not have to go bare foot. I would flush my drugs down the toilet. I would mix it in the carpet under my bed so I wouldn't get caught. Then I'd come down and sit with a flashlight and tweezers picking up pieces to do more lines.

I used to hear the fish tank gurgle of sounds of people outside. I would hear the neighbors laughing at me. I thought there were video cameras recording me and the town was watching me on the news. I would here my dad, my mom, my brothers, my sisters outside my door telling me they loved me. Praying that God would lock me away so I could never hurt anybody, including myself. I would here them leave saying I'm not their brother anymore, I'm not their son anymore. I would lie in a ball in the corner of my room scarred and crying. I would beg for help, but I couldn't stop the drugs. I was too afraid to do the drugs at home, too afraid in the hotel rooms, too afraid in the empty casino buildings, too afraid in my friends houses, too afraid in the car, too afraid in the bar, too afraid after work hours, but I couldn't quit. The drugs owned me. I was no longer Mark. I was something else, somebody else.

I told my best friend that if he was in on it, to just tell me. In on what he would say? Mark, you've gotta quit the drugs. I thought the pizza man was an under-cover cop. I thought women were underage cops trying to get me to have sex with them so they could throw me in jail for sexual crimes. I thought there were people in the trunk of my car. I thought people in restaurants were watching me, taking notes and building a case against me. I thought steak was human flesh, chunks of plaster were rocks of cocaine. I thought people were hiding in the fireplace, behind closed doors, under the bed, in the bushes, the trees, the window seal, coffee stands.

One night I was sitting so scared by myself at my friend's house in the basement. Doing lines and surfing the Internet. I would shut the heater down because every time it kicked on I thought people were breaking in the front door. I was to scared to go upstairs to the refrigerator to get beer. I was to afraid to go upstairs to go to the bathroom. I was too afraid to move. I would hide my dope under the bed mattress and sneak lines in the corner off a CD case in fear of being seen in a windowless basement. I finally went upstairs and sat in the recliner of the empty house. The TV was off and I kept seeing people moving in. Coming from the attic, up the stairs, around the windows, surrounding the doors, the bedrooms, behind the TV, the couch, even under the chairs. I kept telling the cops I would go peacefully to jail. They don't have to gang tackle me or hurt me. The only thing I would ask over and over is to be able to use the bathroom first. I sat for hours pleading for my life and self-sanity, but know would ever bust in the doors.

There were days that I would hide all weekend with a quarter ounce in my room. My roommate would have friends over for parties, to help in the house, to watch football on Sundays and I would lie in my bed to afraid to breathe in fear they would catch me. I would make myself hyperventilate and have to breathe into a towel. I would drip sweat onto my sheets creating a disgusting mix of chemicals and body odor in my room. I would listen to try and hear a pin drop. I would wait for them to leave so I could use the bathroom, take beer out of the refrigerator. I would hide in the shadows of my empty house with all the lights off.

The final few weeks I would hide in the closet. I would park the car in the garage with all the lights off. The neighbors would come over and ask me to come to their house. My roommate and new wife had already left. The house had no furniture left, it was being re-painted and I was not even supposed to be there. I had lost my privilege to live there anymore. It was to be my house but drugs took all my money and I could no longer afford to buy it. No longer afford to rent it.

Shay, Ziad, Joshua, Ty,
Marty,
Anthony and Myself

The Cast of "Karnak and Luxor"

My brother Adam, Mark and Myself

Dave, Jeff, Brian and Myself in Maui for Jeff's wedding in February 2004

Billy Idol and the Lady's Man (okay, they're me)

Jeff, my best friend and new years on the strip in Vegas

XIII

Chemical Dependency Treatment

I pull into Kayla's house about 7pm or so. I eat some soupy noodles, substance for the first time in three days, and had to explain to her why her checking account was being charged $70 in fees, but I have rent money for you. Like that is any conciliation. We watched a documentary. I laughed with her kids for a couple hours, took a long warm shower, and crawled into bed. My father called from his cell phone, which seemed only minutes after I closed my eyes. He was already turning down my street. Great. I threw some jeans and toothpaste in a bag and started the journey to Sundown M Ranch.

The drive over seemed short. I hadn't sat in the same space with just my dad for what seemed forever. We talked. I opened up a little bit. I told him that I think you have to be religious to do the twelve steps of the recovery program. I told him I might not do too well. He said.... if anything at all, this may just be a three week break from life. When you're done, you can return with a clear head. Reading between the lines, it's really a statement without a lot of hope of a better life after treatment.

We slowed down and took the freeway exit off I-82. We passed an apple orchard, a small red bar, and then there was nothing else around. I asked my dad if we were going the right way. As the road wound downward between the mountains and hillside, we were overlooking a cluster of white buildings, red roofs and lots of green grass. Weird, right in the middle of nowhere everything was brown except this set of buildings carved in the valley. "Yeah, that's probably it," I said. We drove down what seemed like a never-ending driveway that had a stationary sign on the right hand side every 10 to 15 feet that read the words; This... Is... The... First... Day... Of... The... Rest... Of... Your... Life. "How cliché," I thought.

The intake process into Sundown M Ranch included an overview of the treatment facility. I sat in the chair across from the intake staff going through my physical withdraws. I had a runny nose, sweaty palms and face, twitches and unable to sit still while I signed the paperwork. "Oh yeah, umm, dad, I don't have any money. You need to give them a credit card for payment." Nice Mark.

I'm officially in chemical dependency treatment and at this point starting to realize how tired I am; emotionally, mentally, physically and spiritually tired. I stayed in the 700-wing for the first five days, which is where incoming and graduating patients stay. It's located within the family building away from the population of patients. My daily schedule included a wake-up announcement over the PA system at 6:45 am, breakfast, morning lecture, group therapy and lunch at 11:45 am. Nice. Then the afternoon repeated the morning with time to use the gym and watch a 12-step recovery program film in the evening. The program was based on the first five steps of the 12-steps of recovery that are:

1. We admitted we were powerless over alcohol - that our lives had become unmanageable.

2. We came to believe that a power greater than ourselves could restore us to sanity.

3. We made a decision to turn our will and our lives over to the care of god, as we understood him.

4. We made a searching and fearless moral inventory of ourselves.

5. We admitted to God, to ourselves, and to another human being the exact nature of our wrongs.

My counselor is a former cocaine addict. We're talking kilos not the teenier or occasional 8-ball that I used. Big leagues. He used to manage car lots and lived in mansions with his sugar mommas. He wore polo's and gold. What I really respected is that he possessed a very good understanding of the alcohol-addicted person. He did not cry in self-pity. Rather, he promoted responsibility and taking charge both of your life and the decisions you will have to make in the recovery process. I like this. He tells it like it is. I think we can work together. Geeze. Am I really interviewing him?

My counselor had me write a journal entry for every day that I was in treatment to let him know where my head was. Hmmm. Where my head was? Here's where my head is, or was, whatever. I lost to all of life's challenges. So please, please do not make me socialize with anybody here. They have never faced or overcome their own challenges in life, yet alone experienced losing to them. They're all low life, lying, cheating, crooks. The only reason they're here is because they're probably on some welfare handout that tax paying citizens, like myself, paid for. They're wasting everyone's time and won't take any of this seriously. For them it's just another stop in life. Why? It's not like they have anywhere else to go. And for good reason, they're the bottom feeders in life. Criminals and Drug addicts that justify their actions because they can't stop using drugs. They lose their kids to Child Protective Services because they choose to get high instead if taking care of their kids. They choose welfare over work because they're lazy. Oh, they have bad hygiene and they stink too. They have failing health from their drug use and poor sexual decisions. They're undereducated, and once they leave, they'll get drunk again. It's inevitable. So, do you still want to know how I am doing?

Allow me to continue, no really, I want too. I'm appalled that I'm being forced to associate with these losers. I'm appalled that I'm sharing a room with one of them. I'm appalled that I can't tell them to quit feeling sorry for themselves. I'm appalled that you think that I can't stay sober. I'm appalled that you think that if I make more than minimum wage, I'll get drunk. I'm appalled that you think if I have a profession, retirement, education, and material possessions that I'll get drunk. I'm appalled that you think if I have friends in my life, that I'll get drunk. Why, because YOU probably will. More importantly, you can't stay sober. You need me to be just as low as you to justify your existence.

Oh, I'm bitter too if you haven't sensed that. Welcome to.... Okay, clear my head. Welcome to treatment. Let's start over. Maybe instead, I'll just write some therapeutic break through in my journal every night until I get out of here. Then I could return to my life and these people could have theirs. That seems to be a better plan. Ya know, there is this saying I heard that I have since adopted as part of my own life. It goes a little something like, "you can blindly go through this process, manipulating your way through. However, isn't that like cheating at solitaire?" Who winds up becoming the loser in the end? What?...ME?

I guess after careful analysis, I ultimately decided to write whatever it was I needed to in my journals, share just enough in group therapy, and interact very little with the patients. In between lectures and group therapy, I took naps. I waited until meals were almost over to get in line so I wouldn't have to wait or sit with anyone. And in the early evenings, I would sit by myself or maybe one other person in the coffee shop. Really just do enough to stay under the radar and get out as soon as possible. This routine occurred like clock work until one of my assignments in group therapy forced me to write a complete inventory of all the negative things I'd ever done.

Much to my surprise, I started getting into the assignment as it turned to assigning dollar values to the things I stole, used, took, spent and lost through my drug use. I held nothing back on this assignment. Yeah. Let's see. If I live until the ripe old age of 90, my work would have provided me a retirement that would have been worth approximately $7.5 million based on my annual salary at work with overtime and expense reimbursement that totaled about $70,000. At the early age of 53, I would have been eligible to draw from my retirement contributions. There were also my consulting contracts with the casino. Hmmmm? Six new casinos, approximately $9 million in financing multiplied by say 4% or so, is about $360,000 in consulting fees.

Maybe a small residual of say 3%, multiplied by $2 million annual net revenue, times six new casinos is a residual of also $360,000 per year. Furthermore there were my non-profit contracts for casino fundraising that I was allowed to make $10,000 per month. Man, life was just about to get good. Do the math, do the math. Ouch. Did I really give this up? Unfortunately I was still so toxic that this really just swelled my ego. Keep writing. Say more. You're the man! Sick. Sick. Sick.

How much have I already spent to the disease? Drugs, alcohol, gambling, cars, frauds, paychecks. Wow, almost $565,000 since I turned 18. What about all the people I hurt along the way? Suddenly I was forced to realize that part of that grand total included checks, credit cards, vehicles, gas, money and food that I had stolen from my dad and step-mom. Part of it included using each sibling for shelter and loans. Part of it included gambling debts I forced upon my brother when I had a checking account in his name, as well as the gambling debts I incurred in my own name, and the gambling debts to people that I had borrowed money and never paid back. Part of that amount included a number of crimes that locked me behind bars for almost a year of my life from the age of 18 through 22. I started feeling pretty shitty. Why did I do this to people? Why did I steal when I did not need anything? Why did I hurt people and take away from them emotionally and materially?

I reached out a little bit. I started smoking cigarettes with the others. I started showing up to meals and eating with groups of people. I started working on my daily journals with others in the coffee shop. I started staying up late talking and getting to know why the others were in treatment. To my surprise, I really wasn't that different. They were really just like me. More importantly, I was like them: hurt and never wanting the world to hurt me again. I started opening up in group. I started looking at the little boy that lost his life when he was abandoned at the age of two. I started feeling all those pains again that I had long forgotten; the feelings of rejection and not being good enough in this world. Not good enough for the simple fact that my own family wouldn't keep me.

I started realizing what treatment is. I started seeing what a godsend my counselor is. I started learning that my body is chemically different than that of other people. I crave the dopamine release within my brain that is chemically triggered by drugs, alcohol, gambling, crime, and sex (maybe not even in that order). I started understanding that my drug use is in fact a reaction from suppressing internal feelings that I did not want to process. These unprocessed feelings cause major anguish; on top of my chemical makeup and physical cravings, now I have developed mental and emotional cravings for a medication that hides all unresolved feelings. Hmmm, I guess I have some work to do.

So what is treatment? For me treatment really boiled down to 21 days of badly needed clean time, education of how my body works and rejects alcohol, answers to why I did the bad things I did while under the influence of alcohol, and finally, guidance on how to go forward. Pointing blame to just the disease of alcoholism, seemed irresponsible, considering what I know from my experiences and education. Not taking true responsibility for the things I did, felt like an easy way out. I know why others place blame. Most people who have become chemically dependant come from families with histories of mental, physical, sexual and emotional abuse. They've never been taught to work, pay bills or obey laws. Probation and welfare is "normal life". To go into treatment and have someone tell you it's not normal, may be too overwhelming for them. They may not even understand; they've never known another world outside of that. For them, to trust that all their irregular, deviant behaviors are the lies from the disease of alcoholism, may be the most effective way to get them to listen, and trust a counselor in order to try a new way in life: not drinking, not stealing, not lying, paying bills and slowly claiming ownership for their actions. Otherwise they are too sensitive to have to accept all at once that despite alcohol, they made these decisions. I think that is the long-term reality if we stay sober long enough. What's my part in it?

So, for me this is simply step one. I've been in too many places and seen too much in work and college to place all blame on a disease called alcoholism, as an end all for my negative behavior. I know the decisions I made and the feelings I was protecting when I made them. I wanted people to feel how hurt I was inside. I wanted to hurt people because of the way I felt inside. I wanted to push people away to give me a reason to sit in self-misery, empty and all alone. Alcoholism. No, too easy of a way out for me, is what I thought. Or is it exactly the disease of alcoholism?

Now step two in recovery. My counselor says, "Mark, do you know why your parents are coming to family therapy?" "Yeah, they have to. It's part of treatment," I respond. "No, because they love you," reminds my counselor. My eyes start to tear up. It's hard to believe, and I don't want to accept that anyone loves me, especially my parents whom I've hurt so much. I spent an entire life punishing them for hurting me. He says, "Try not to defend anything and let them say what they need to." The hardest reality of the whole thing is that they are not the only parents I have hurt. There is another set that includes my adopted mother. There is yet another set that includes the biological family that I am at this point starting to consciously remember, as I began to sober up. I love. I miss. I'm confused. I don't know what to feel. Suck it up though. You know who'll be here for family counseling Mark.

The next two and a half days were so intense. Family counseling included endless tears over the words written on paper that my father, my stepmother and I took turns reading from. I had so much anger and peace, all at the same time. I wanted to say that I hate you for making me feel this way. But I also wanted to let those feelings go, for the first time, and embrace their love. I felt my father's love. I felt my stepmother's love. Her and I cried the most. It's truly amazing too live so full of hate, yet cry from the inner most parts of your soul when you hear the words, "I love you." This is my single most significant changing point in recovery. I went back to my counselor and asked, "What do I need to do?" He says, "Mark, you need to go to an Oxford home," he says. "What is an Oxford home?"

My counselor explained what an oxford home was. I also attended one of the presentations for oxford houses, and read some literature to familiarize myself. Apparently, in 1988, Congress enacted P.L. 100-690, the Anti-Drug Abuse Act. This Act includes a provision requiring all states to establish a revolving loan fund to provide start-up funds for groups wishing to open sober living environments.

There are four major types of sober living environments:

1. Oxford Houses
2. Taylor Houses
3. Clean and Sober Houses
4. Transitional Housing

Shared living is designed to facilitate an environment that is normally run by other people in recovery that promote eventual self-sufficiency and re-entry back into society. Monthly rent range within the $2/300 hundred range depending whether you share space or have your own room.

Oxford Houses:

Houses are long-term with rehabilitative support for individuals that want to quit drinking and using drugs. Individual houses are part of a private, non-profit organization whose chapters are located throughout the world. They hold meetings that are weekly for individual houses, quarterly for chapters and annual for the organization as a whole. Houses are self-supporting and are not owned, operated or funded by the state, federal governments or private homeowners like a halfway house, transitional or any other type of recovery type living. The houses are either all male or all female. There is a combination of single and shared rooms. Monthly rent is all inclusive and includes utilities, cable, telephone and staples (coffee, minimal food, etc.).

Houses are democratically run by other recovering alcoholics and drug addicts with no professional staff. There are secretary, treasurer, president.... positions that are held by the members of the house for a six month term. Weekly meetings include financial status reports, house chore reports, and a reading of one of the 12-oxford house traditions.

New house members require a 2/3 majority vote. General expectations for living include house chores, weekly house meetings, abstinence from drugs and alcohol, and no disruptive behavior. Although there are no requirements, a strong recovery program to include after care appointments, obtaining a sponsor and attending 12-Step Recovery Program meetings is strongly suggested, as is eventual employment.

Disruptive behavior may result in corrective action leading to dismissal if confirmed by a 51% house vote. Suspected drug use by two or more house members requires a mandatory UA. Refusal of the UA or any drug or alcohol use results in immediate removal from the house. Generally the person has one hour to leave. Otherwise, there is no restriction on an individual's length of stay.

There is an 11pm curfew during the weekdays and 1 am curfew during the weekends for the first 30 days. Overnight guests are generally limited to two nights a week after the first 30 days. Any deviations to this have to be approved by the other members of the house.

Taylor Houses:

Predominately women and co-ed living. The minimum stay is 30 days with a two week written notice for move out. The house is run by a "house advisor". There are weekly chores and house meetings. Nonparticipation results in a $20 fine. The "house advisor" must approve any over night journeys from the house. Otherwise, you're restricted to a 10 pm curfew for the first 30 days. Overnight guests are limited to one night a week and must be approved by the other house members. If you fail to work a program or provide proof of 12-Step Recovery Program attendance when asked, fail a random UA, or display disruptive behavior, you'll be asked leave.

Clean and Sober Houses:

Housing is normally a limited liability corporation that is run by a manager. Funding is offset by state and federal grants, tax credits, investing partners and resident rent. Members of the house live together as a family unit and provide support for each other in early recovery programs. Everyone is equal and disputes are resolved with a house meeting – majority rules.

Transitional Housing:

Housing is available for persons waiting to be released from custody, persons in recovery from drugs and alcohol, or people just needing a transitional place to live. They are male, female and co-ed living. Some houses also provide space for parents with children. Houses are generally self-owned and individual rules are adopted by the homeowner. For example, some require a minimum length of sobriety, others require minimum hours of weekly employment, others require mandatory 12-Step Recovery Program attendance, sponsor and after care involvement, and some just require the monthly rent. A typical room will house two or three beds, and the house can provide space for up to fourteen people.

Of the four choices, the Oxford House seemed to be the right choice. My counselor tells me to just do the interview with the members of the house, and leave the rest in God's hands. God's hands, I thought, not mine. Interview? Huh? Apparently I have to interview with the members of the house. Okay, how do I do that? Of the three male oxford homes in Yakima there is only one opening. It's in the Summit View Oxford House. It was opened about a year and a half ago. It has seven bedrooms and holds nine people (two shared rooms and five single rooms). Okay. There are approximately 55 male patients at Sundown M Ranch, maybe a dozen or so graduating, and 3-5 needing housing in Yakima. My chances seemed to be okay.

I did the interview on the evening of May 2nd, 2005, one day before I was scheduled to complete inpatient treatment. They asked questions about my source for rent, whether I had a car, a license, would I work, would I attend 12-Step Recovery Program meetings and get a sponsor, would I participate with house chores, meetings and be an active house member, what was my drug history and do I want to be sober? Yes, yes, and yes. They accepted me. I was on the next phase of my recovery journey.

In the afternoon of May 3, 2005, I met with the outpatient coordinators at Sundown M Ranch. What they recommended was 90 days of weekly after care appointments at the ranch. Good I thought: I could stay at the Oxford home, do the after care appointments and then resume normal life. Oh, and go to 90, 12-step recovery program meetings in 90 days and get a sponsor. Wait. What? Sponsor? What exactly is a sponsor? A sponsor is someone who has shown personal success in the recovery process and then supports other recovering alcoholics through the 12-steps of recovery. A sponsor does not enforce rules or require a certain type of living; they merely support and offer opinions when asked. Seems great, if your self-motivated and have enough already in your bag of life experiences to draw from. The reality is a lot of drug abusers don't. All aspects of their lives were placed on pause when they began using drugs. For many it means never developing an interpersonal relationship, holding a job, paying bills, or being self-reliant. They need much more assistance than the occasional atta boy phone call from a sponsor. I need much more assistance.

However, the fine line is standing on your own two feet and asking for assistance from your sponsor, but not becoming codependent in a way that allows your sponsor take too much control of your life. You possess the ability to know when this line is crossed. For the master chess players, it creates a future point of blame if things don't improve. Don't cheat yourself. It's not a game anymore.

XIV

Oxford House

On May 23, 2004, which is also my father's 54th birthday, I was leaving treatment for the real world. We stopped in a little restaurant outside of Yakima, Washington. I had a nice steak and shrimp and a Pepsi for the first time in over three weeks. The drive back to my parent's home was about three hours, and we had a lot of catching up to do. When we drove through Tacoma I started feeling a little queasy. We were driving through and physically seeing the buildings and streets that reminded me of many of the terrible and disgusting things I had done. We finally made it to my parent's home. I had a lot of things to do over the next couple days. I needed to move all of my stuff from Kayla's house, gather up all my mail, cash my final payroll checks, and oh yeah, put together a desk for my parent's home office.

So I move into the Oxford Home on May 25th 2004. Wow. Here I go. It's a brown house with nine housemates, seven bedrooms, four bathrooms, three refrigerators, two living rooms and now me. My initial thought was how dirty it was; probably germs all over the place and everyone smokes like chimneys. C'mon Mark, you can do this; it's only temporary, right? For the next 90-days of my life, I was to live in the Oxford home with eight other recovering alcoholics, attend 90, 12-

step recovery program meetings, and get a sponsor to walk me through the 12-steps of recovery, attend 12-aftercare weekly appointments for an hour and a half at Sundown M Ranch, and attend weekly sessions with a cognitive behavioral therapist to treat my compulsive gambling. 90,12,12,90… my head was a blur. Just go forward!

Emotionally, at this point, I think I am ready. Financially, well, lets recap why I am here. I have drugged, boozed, gambled and partied away every dollar I have ever earned, except for my final payroll checks. So really, I have no money. If I tally up what it will cost me to live in recovery. Let's see. Hmmm. Monthly rent is $260, cobra insurance is $370, psychologist co-pay is $280, and aftercare appointment co-pay is $50. That's $960 a month to live in a recovery house. How am I supposed to do this? I can't imagine how people that have exhausted all their resources could possibly do this. Maybe already set up to fail? I'll make it though. 90-days. C'mon Mark. Just don't be a moron and spend money you don't have. You can do this.

So I ride with a couple of my new housemates, Jay and Tyrone, to my first 12-step recovery program meeting. Jay has a soft heart, but at times can be a little peculiar. He's in his late 50's, about 5'7", balding and slightly over weight. He has a cast on his left forearm; his trophy for wrecking the company van of his former employer where he worked as a chemical dependency counselor. He was fired, denied un-employment and was charged with a DUI. He is a very closed guy. Spends a lot of time in his room. He did have a van though. He said he felt that was his gift from God in recovery. His job was to take people to self-help meetings.

Tyrone is a 19-year-old kid from Auburn. He was into selling, snorting and smoking methamphetamine. He dropped out of high school and has been in and out of juvenile detention his entire life. Not a lot of parental involvement in his early years. Really, he's doing the only thing he was ever taught, selling drugs and getting high.

We arrive at the meeting hall and sit against the wall in a small room where they close the doors for an hour and everyone lights a cigarette. A guy walks around the room serving coffee, as the meeting chair asks people to share whether they have a sobriety birthday, which is really acknowledgement for being free of drugs and alcohol for predetermined lengths of time. The chair also asks for sobriety announcements and if anyone would like to volunteer to sponsor a newcomer. The chair selects someone to read a topic from a 12-step recovery book. People are then randomly selected to share how the topic read affects their lives.

Most people don't share on the topic. They take their five minutes to talk about what's pissing them off in life right now by revealing the drama and chaos that results from over-reacting to the littlest of things. There are also those, well a majority of the members that share how bad they want to get drunk or high. Inevitably some of them do, and they call that a relapse. I'm still new in this process; at this point I call this a poor decision and lack of self-control. As I sift through the smoke filled room to make eye contact with the ones sharing. I think to myself that my commitment in Yakima to complete outpatient is going to be a very long 90-days. Gulp!

At the close of the meeting I asked this tattooed guy to be my sponsor. No problem, doing the drill. I'll be able to report to outpatient that I already have a sponsor. In reality though, my new sponsor is a well known for habitual relapses and currently has well under six months of sobriety. But what do I care, I only have 89 days left.

After the meeting Jay is already in his red van waiting for us. Tyrone and I start walking out and this curly haired, thick glasses, overweight guy with his pants falling off his waist, sticks out his hand and says, "my name's Gerry, what's yours?" Ummm, Mark, I reply. And he says it again, and again, and again, and he won't let go of my hand. I try to pull away and his face changes. He puts his arms around my neck and pushes his weight of about 250 pounds on me. I look up from the ground, my arms are extended and hands to my side, He's laying on me, foam on the side of his mouth, and his hand balled in a fist getting ready to punch me.

Although I lay still, what I was thinking inside is, "whatever, I just don't want anyone to think I picked on the retard!" Tyrone grabs his arm and pulls him off me. We stand up, his face changes, and he sticks out his hand and says, "my name's Gerry, what's yours?" I finally leave. Later my new sponsor told me that he was a very good-looking, high school athlete until someone slipped acid in his beer at a party; he never came back mentally. I have to ask myself at this point whether I really even care, and that answer I'm not sure of yet. I guess I'm really in a little shock. Welcome to the 12-step recovery program. Maybe I should find a new meeting; perhaps non-smoking and no, well, you get the idea.

So the guys in the house aren't exactly people that I'd have chosen to associate myself with in my prior life, nonetheless, each has a sad story. The majority, sorry to say have parents that emotionally, mentally and in some case, even physically neglected then as children. Although a parent figure may have been around; emotionally they were abandoned before they even had a fighting chance, an unfortunate commonality. However, once you're able to get beyond the "I'm pissed off at the world" barrier, they are some of the neatest, sensitive, and caring people you'll ever meet. That's if their self-absorbency time schedule allows the time to meet you.

Dale is in his early 40's; he's a former musician from a local band. He had spent three years in prison for cooking methamphetamine. Now he's been living in the Oxford home for the past two years trying to put his life back together. Also he is a counselor in training for the youth facility at a chemical dependency treatment center. It seems he's really a small child trapped in an adult body to afraid to step out of the safety provided in his current living arrangements. Inside he's emotionally crippled, and always working on ways to keep his frustration in check. More times than not he loses to the little things that cause friction in his world.

Intellectually he's very smart, he knows this. He can be a great manipulator by using emotional issues of others. However, when used wisely, he has an ability to lead a person down the path to discovering their inner pain. He helped me with two major issues: controlling my reactions to Abbey's venting of her uncontrollable desire to always want to use drugs, and letting go of the pain from Mark's suicide that I didn't even realize I was harboring inside.

The State of Washington garnishes half Dale's wage for back child support. However, he receives a monthly trust fund check from his parents to help pay his bills. He's a little on the hefty side, and his health has been compromised from his drug use days. He was recently hospitalized for a mild heart attack, but he still smokes. He has a girlfriend that he met on the Internet; they spend time together once a week. Otherwise his nights are filled with classes at the community college towards his chemical dependency certificate, playing video games, listening to music, and playing his guitar.

Although Dale doesn't attend the12-step recovery program meetings or have a sponsor, he seems to have curbed his desire to want to use drugs and alcohol. At one point we have to ask ourselves if this accomplishment is enough on its own?

Then there is Joaquin, hmmm, Joaquin is very reserved and gives a perception that it's okay for people to walk all over him. Also he's a reformed methamphetamine smoker. He is almost 30 years old and a little on the heavy side. His parents were non-existent during his childhood because he grew up having to boil water to take showers, brush his teeth, and even stitched his own clothes. He was raised by and consequently very hurt by his uncle who never stopped long enough to see what was going on with Joaquin. A parental responsibility, yes, unfortunately his uncle assumed that role.

He had his heart broken by a woman during the end of his drug using days and has had a hard time letting that go. He's very insecure and easily intimidated. But he knows this. He keeps himself in check by distancing himself from others and not allowing too many people to hurt him. Although he doesn't attend the 12-step recovery program meetings or has a sponsor, he too seems to have curbed his desire to want to use drugs and alcohol. When you peel away his pains, he has a heart of gold and very caring. His ability to absorb other people emotionally by exercising tolerance and patience is his gift to the world.

Joaquin has lived in the Oxford home for almost two years. Also he's the Chapter Chair and is responsible for expanding Oxford's Services, locating new homes and finding long-term housing for people in recovery.

Lynn is a 37-year-old grandfather from Chelan, Washington.

Who was also abandoned by his biological family and later adopted as a small child. His drug of choice is marijuana. The State of Washington garnishes half his employment earnings for back child support for his 20-year-old daughter. He has an enormous amount of court fines, restitution, and will probably not have a driver's license for the next 5-7 years until these debts are all paid off. He plays the martyr, woe is me, why does the world keep dumping on me? He continues this role by doing just enough to stay one step behind in life. Lynn also has a heart of gold, who would give you his arm if you needed it. He's very insightful and extremely active in his 12-step recovery program. He is a man waiting to stand on his own two feet if the world would only let him, baggage and all.

Eli is a local boy from Yakima; and is a very sensitive 19-year-old kid that dropped out of school in the 10th grade. He plays the poor me card that tend to leave him sulking in his own self-pity because people can never meet his expectations. Although, he just forgets to tell you what those expectations are. He's very smart and has an uncanny ability to see the end result or the way a particular event will ultimately pan out. Unfortunately he doesn't give people enough time to walk down the path of self-discovery. So he just doesn't allow them the opportunity to experience the journey and understand life's lessons. He will be very successful with people when he learns to lead as a mentor and help people through guided discovery to the answers he already knows. Allowing them to gain wisdom through their own experience. Nonetheless, the frustration of not understanding his talents, or the limitations of others; causes a temper tantrum because he cannot understand why people cannot see what he thinks he knows.

Eli is also starting school to earn credits towards his GED and associate of arts degree simultaneously. Also he has a pending court matter for eluding cops in a high speed drunken driving chase and assault. Eli has a sponsor and attends the 12-step recovery program meetings. I think that he is Kind of the sad puppy dog without a lot of friends. This guy really likes neat pens. Inside he expresses himself through writing things on paper that he never shares with others. What was his biggest source of pain? When he was 11 years old he was jumped and beaten by three strangers and then wanted to hurt society for not protecting him ever since.

Vince is 19-years-old. His father is a multi-millionaire orchard owner. He went to treatment for smoking dope, or more politically correct, marijuana. He has a sponsor and attends the 12-step recovery program meetings and really doesn't mind being here. Vince never really had to do much in life and knows that when he's done with the outpatient treatment, he can go back home to work for his father. Otherwise, he stays out of the daily dramas that seem to engulf so many others. So he spends a majority of his time playing on-line interactive video games in his room.

Mike was abandoned by his biological family and adopted as a small child. He was informed that his biological mother died a week before he was scheduled to re-unite with her for the first time. Also he killed his friend in a drunk driving accident when he was 16 years old. The shame from the abandonment leaves him unappreciative of his adopted family. Then his guilt over killing his best friend keeps him emotionally crippled. All those feelings combined left him smoking crack with a loaded shotgun hanging from his mouth when he was 42 years old and then crawled to his family's home crying for help. They rescued him just like before as an abandoned child. Only this time they sent him to chemical dependency treatment; which is the first step in recovery.

Mike has lived his entire life too afraid of letting you see his internal pains. Consequently, he bottles up these feelings that ultimately make it harder and harder to ever communicate in fear of saying something wrong and being abandoned all over again. As a result the emotions and feelings boil up until he snaps. He doesn't have a sponsor and doesn't attend the 12-step recovery program meetings. Instead he rather searches for a woman to be in control of his decision-making, and then complains about her later; which then pushes her out of his life. A vicious cycle for a guy that is really in search of the mom figure he lost as a child. In result his emotional growth that controls his outward decision-making capacity is not much more than that of an 8-year old child.

Mike started smoking crack and drinking again. I can't pinpoint the specific time, but after about 10-months of his own sobriety, he stole a very expensive bracelet from me and hawked it for dope. Mike was last seen being dropped off at a detox facility, which is a place to sober up. He put the dagger through his parent's heart with this relapse. I hope he finds his way back.

Chad is the complete womanizer. At the age of 36 this is the first time he's ever lived away from his parent's home, well other than jail that is. He went to chemical dependency treatment at James Oldham Treatment Center for really his 7th or 8th time. He had also spent three years in prison for home burglaries, and he's a heroin addict. Chad knows what he wants and doesn't spend a lot of time dealing with other people's feelings; more or less put up or shut up. He has a sponsor and attends the 12-step recovery program meetings regularly. The day after his 9-month birthday of being free of drugs and alcohol, Chad started shooting heroin again. He was last seen entering a detox facility in Seattle, Washington after a four-month binge with heroin.

Ronald is 42-years-old and originally from Georgia. His wife divorced him and his family has since lost all confidence in Ronald. He's a late stage alcoholic who relapsed early on during the post inpatient treatment recovery process. Then he was extradited from Yakima to the Port Townsend jail to serve a six to nine month sentence for violating his probation with booze.

Joe is a 33-year-old fisherman from the State of Alaska. He's intelligent and rebounds quickly in the fishing industry. However, he is a late stage alcoholic that would drink to oblivion every night with Maybe 1-2 fifths of liquor. Joe relapsed in the first week while living at the Oxford house. We have no idea of his current whereabouts.

Ty is another 19-year-old from Auburn, Washington. After living with us for a month we voted him out for disruptive behavior; more specifically, he was stealing from the house. He relapsed shortly after moving back in with his family. He has an awesome singing voice if he could just find his way through the maze of hopelessness.

Bill is a 20-year-old basketball player. Who currently works as a telemarketer in hopes to play professional ball one day. Bill unfortunately relapsed and moved into another clean and sober home.

Juan is 27-years-old from the State of Montana. I shared a

room in the Oxford house with him. Juan was in and out of the Oxford home fairly quickly; I would say maybe five to six months? He has been successful thus far at maintaining his sobriety considering he was a prior IV drug user. While living at the Oxford house, he contacted all his old bill collectors and made arrangements to pay them back. He quit smoking cigarettes in September 2004. Also he contacted the courts in Montana and faced his pending legal charges. These charges were dismissed as he provided proof of successfully completing chemical dependency treatment. Juan eventually moved in with his fiancé who is also from Montana as well. She arrived in Yakima three weeks earlier then Juan to start her treatment process. Also they're getting married on May 5, 2005. He's very mellow person and does not get wrapped up in the 12-step recovery program drama that often preoccupies so many others. He is a perfect example of admitting defeat and doing the hard things in life to reclaim control. He has become one of my closest friends.

Remember Tyrone, the 19-year-old kid I mentioned earlier? He eventually relapsed. He had left a voicemail saying, "don't relapse, I'm going to prison." Then his sponsor relapsed on heroin on his own 8-year sobriety birthday; Tyrone's relapse was shortly after. We never know who's following our lead, or do we?

Welcome to my new housemates, my new home, and my new life. As part of my aftercare recommendation from Sundown M Ranch, I made arrangements to see a cognitive behavioral therapist to treat my compulsive gambling. Since I no longer had a valid driver's license or car at that time, I had the fine pleasure of walking every Wednesday to see my Psychologist. My first appointment was introductory, so just really getting to know my therapist. A neat coincidence was that he was related to one of the co-founders of YWAM. Hmmm, the degrees of separation in life are very small. I was really excited to tell my mother about this.

In my first few sessions, we identified self-defeating behaviors and identified healthier options. Also my therapist encouraged that I should develop positive decision-making skills. As part of my therapy I was instructed to write an autobiography of my life with the details of all the hurt and pain. This task became the focal point of my therapy sessions. During the sessions a significant amount of time was spent over the next 16-weeks was on page one, which was my abandonment as a child. My therapist had communicated some things I've never listened long enough to hear before. He said Mark; your life is like that of Moses' beginning. When the Philistines were ordered by the king Pharaoh to kill all Hebrew male children, Moses was placed in a basket, swept down stream and his life was sparred. For whatever reason, your biological mom kept you against the laws of Korean culture until you were almost two years old. Then she placed you on the steps of a police station, which probably broke more laws. She risked her own life to put me in a place that may have even been safer than a church given the circumstances. Why, because a police officer has a societal obligation to place me in an orphanage. He kept telling me how lucky I am to be alive. How does rejected and lucky fit in the same sentence? Do people understand how hard these words are to hear when you've lived an entire life of shame by being abandoned? Guilt by all the pain you've caused to others trying to deny this shame? I do. But maybe I'm wrong. Maybe I'm willing to find that out.

We had a couple sessions where he started to tear up. He said that he practices psychology to help people, but his real heart is in ministry and a faith based recovery. He also works with over-seas adoptions. My therapist said he knows it's not an accident that our lives have crossed and that he understands why he is doing what he does. Wow that was overwhelming for me. So I ask myself, "God, what is your plan for my life?"

So I have to recap at this point; I'm no longer employed, no car, claimed bankruptcy, no license, and I'm living in a clean and sober home with 8-other guys. What a realization for me! To make this even better, after a couple weeks of meetings I heard through the grapevine my sponsor relapsed. Well I guess that explains why he would never return my messages; he was out getting high! Suddenly my new hopes and dreams in recovery have started with an over-medicated guy throwing me to the ground and my sponsoring relapsing. I started thinking I was going to have to fight my way out of a trap that others in recovery are okay being in. The trap is of just existing only within the confinement of a recovery world.

So I made a list of requirements for my next new sponsor.

This person had to have values, morals, come from destitute and made something of his life, have a family, education, employed, and be an active volunteer. Most importantly, he had to be strong in his conviction and know recovery intellectually. I think I was secretly convinced that there is no such person that's exists within the 12-step recovery Program. Really, consider the resumes of Reformed drunks that stole to get their booze. I went on an active search, and attended the numerous 12-step recovery program meetings, and talked with a lot of people. Inevitably they all confirmed what I thought I knew. Which was that they were all whiner's that created chaos out of the littlest of situations, and lacked the ability to even see that within themselves. Negativity before treatment. And now negativity within the recovery process. It's difficult sometimes to separate help from harm when you are so vulnerable.

My opinion was that most of the counselors and people in the 12-step recovery programs are under-educated and have no work background, except for stealing things, getting caught, going to jail, becoming reformed, and now giving others directions for healthy living. Is this the best lead to follow? Sounds negative but in reality a 12-step recovery program is the best thing and perhaps the only thing that most of these people have in their life. Mentally and emotionally they are kids and in fact a large majority have never even held a steady job before. Most don't have a GED and assume welfare is part of life. I hope I was wrong and just feeling negative.

So I was becoming frustrated with the 12-step recovery program and really didn't care to much to find commonalities with the people there. Instead I used my five minutes of sharing time to state why my life was better in some shape or form. Hmmm, I see a psychologist once a week so I don't need any of you. I have a four-year degree in accounting and almost two more years of marketing. Also I have a very marketable resume. So back off! Wait, you or me? What am I even proving?

It's now mid-July and I'm writing in my journal every night trying to understand what the heck I am doing. I had attended the 12-step recovery programs religiously. I was Searching, looking, but for what? One evening Phil stops by towards the end of a meeting that I'm attending. He's Tyrone's sponsor, and yes, the guy I had issues with from the previous meeting hall regarding our disputes over intellectualizing the program. We went for a burger at a restaurant where he gave me his telephone number and a compact disc of Scott. Scott is a prominent businessman from Los Angeles that speaks on the 12-step recovery programs and it's impact on his life. So I agree to go to Moxee, Washington next Friday to attend a meeting with him, where there are a large number of the members that have at least 20-years of sobriety.

Phil may be good for me since he is very intellectual and challenging. He even mentioned the way smart people test things to prove points to themselves. An example, my ability to pick one of the people best known for relapsing in recovery as my sponsor. This is someone that had already relapsed twice in the past six months. When he relapsed all it did was prove a point to myself that the program of recovery doesn't work. However, it's about sobriety and fellowship, and slowing down the disease. I have to stop trying to prove myself right and just work the steps with a sponsor. I need a sponsor; maybe not Phil, but perhaps he and I can attend different meetings in search of one. He knows this and I know this; this is our destiny with each other. No luck though, I just need to Keep moving forward and that's all I can do. In the back of my head the lingering question becomes more and more real. Does a sponsor for me exist in Yakima? Do I exist in Yakima?

My first weekly after care appointment was at 6pm at Sundown. It was with a group of about 12-15 people. Our time was really spent on sharing how our week has gone; the good and the bad. The focus was really to keep us in the now, the present day events and also to keep us focused on what we can do. I wasn't really impressed at first it felt like it was just more of 12-step recovery program mumble jumble. What I heard was hi, my name is so and so and my life sucks. I can't get a job, I wanna get high, so what's the point. The state sucks because they won't give me my kid and I can't drive for 3-years cause this stupid ignition interlock. Hmmm. Let's see if I understand correctly. You were arrested for selling methamphetamines and Child Protective Services took your kids because you went to jail. Also the kid doesn't even know who their real father is. The last real job you had been at some burger joint where even there they wouldn't let you work in front of people. Your only job skill is that you know at this point you have none. Your license is revoked because you hit a parked police car leaving the bar with a .28 blood alcohol content. Well, maybe that was not actually said. The reality is that I have to apologize because whoever told you getting sober meant free handouts lied to you. Staying sober means its time to clean up all of life's problems and so buck up and get a strong support group. Yes, the floodgate of life's problems that we drank and drugged to pretend never existed, is now right in front of our very eyes. It is now time to deal with it.

So, during my second after care appointment I ran into Abbey who is 26 years old from Baring. She has twin kids that live with her ex-husband. She has a very outgoing personality and was formerly employed as a cocktail waitress at a local bar. She was at Sundown M Ranch during my last week of treatment. She is very beautiful with a strong personality. We became friends and started hanging out. We went to all night coffee shops and attended the 12-step recovery program meetings together. I spent a lot of time at her house getting to know her mother who is here from Barring for three months, and her two kids, they're great. Abbey took me to Tacoma for my bankruptcy hearing. (Sorry, part of my clean up process) As our friendship progresses some things became verbally combative. I really felt she had too much pre-occupation with wanting to get high. Get over it your life is chaotic. You're jeopardizing my recovery, is what I thought. Only later in recovery is when I understood how valuable her friendship is and how she only verbalizes what most don't. This doesn't make her any more or less stable. Now my role becomes improving my ability to look past this and not to own any of her issues, rather being there for support as she figures out these areas on her journey. That's when I realized what friendship is. Why, because she would also do the same for me. At that time I just didn't realize how high maintenance I would become during this phase of inter-personal development.

Stacy, who is my roommate Juan's girlfriend, wanted me to meet her roommate Rebekah. Rebekah is a former model from Los Angeles and her mother lives in New York. She's very beautiful and as you'll read to find out, became one of my better friends in recovery.

So one night I was at the house eating top ramen and shrimp. That really was about the extent of what I can cook. Juan, Stacy and Rebekah walked in the house. They are on their way to play softball in the one of the 12-step recovery program leagues. My first impression was that she was a little quirky and thin. She was wearing a red hat, blue t-shirt and blue jumpsuit. She extended her hand and introduced herself and right then there was an instant attraction from me to her. I didn't know what it was though because part of me felt it was my loneliness and desire to be with a female at a deeper level. The other part of me felt like I could see through her. She was trying to be self-confident yet her shoulders were slumped and timid body language said she was real meek and vulnerable. I thought looking past her fronts there is a real neat person in there and I wanted to know her. I went to play softball with them, but yet had so much false pride on my part though. The reason was I wearing a $1,200 gold bracelet, Gucci sunglasses, an orange polo shirt, and khaki shorts. Yeah, all for just playing softball. What a dork!

As we're riding in the back of Stacy's car, Rebekah became willing to share. She offered me a cigarette. I'm trying to quit and I really was never a smoker, but I had one. Who is she? A scared little girl who had been hurt bad. She uses her beauty to draw guys in that ultimately take advantage of her. That hurts her because she secretly wants a friend to trust. But if a guy turns down her advances she feels all the shame and rejection from the hurt she's experienced as a child. What a vicious cycle.

We play catch in the softball field. Take turns batting and giving each other high fives. It's time to go and we race to the car. Whoa, who am I? Why am I so comfortable that I just let down my guard? I ran like a child free from all my pain. Who is she? How did she just do this to me? As we're driving back you talk with this major front, I'm from LA, I'm a model, ... I didn't really listen much. All I saw was your body language. Your eyes weren't confident, but your posture was closed. You were so terrified of letting anyone in. Don't try and know me is the vibe I got. You can never know me. That's what the empty glow, the small scowl on her forehead, the dashing eyes looking for acceptance from everyone said to me. She's damaged and She wants to cry her pain away but she's been down this road before. She knows where it goes, back to the same empty being. She wants to be free to live, but she won't trust anyone though, she can't. The road ends where it starts, disappointment. She'll play everyone just to fall into her trap just so she can say see, I told you so. Watch out Mark! That's what I knew at the time.

A couple weeks went by and a group of us went to a local bowling alley. She was real flashy; changing her shirt trying to get everyone's attention. Don't get me wrong. She is very beautiful, she is thin, has curves, strong facial features, brunette, soft eyes, and full lips. Physically she is as perfect as I ever dreamed of someone could be. As she worked so hard to get the attention of everyone in the bowling alley, including the guys in the next lane. That's fine because we're not dating. God, she's so much like me though, she needs them to acknowledge her to fill her empty void of affection from others. She just needs them for her self-esteem. Great, just like me and I understand this behavior. It doesn't even bother me even though it's unhealthy but at this point it doesn't bother me.

Another week or so goes by. I go to the clean and sober home that she is living in. We talk till about 1am about past lives, who we knew, where we lived, what we lost, what kind of drugs we did. It was really a superficial conversation. One I'm so comfortable talking about because losing things externally doesn't really faze me. Actually is a stroke to my ego to tell people my life experiences, it is so shallow of me, I know. It meant nothing for me to talk about things I cared nothing about in the first place. The conversation slowly moves towards the reality of living lives that we never had our hearts into in the first place yet continued down the path of complete self-destruction always searching for something. We just didn't know what it was we were searching for. Despite dying inside everyday, this small hope for something kept us alive. What were people like us searching for? I don't know, but I never gave up looking. I was beginning to believe that neither did she.

Then we talked of the fantasy of wanting kids and a family. All of a sudden my heart melts. That is the secret dream in me that never died despite how bad my life got. I know now what I was searching for; I was searching for love. I didn't even have to know her anymore because I already found what it was I've been looking for; someone to share my dream with. No longer the superficial dream of a

Brady bunch family, but the dream of love and family to erase all the painful memories that our pasts are filled with. Now it was time to really to love and be loved unconditionally, to hold and be held never let go.

In those few short days my heart in so many ways, already belonged to her. My quest in recovery was now changed and became an inner search within myself to become a complete person to be able to prove to her I was for real. To prove to her I could be her best friend and maybe one-day life partner. I had a lot of work to do and I even read relationship books to understand the opposite sex. However, these dreams that I had, blinded me to some of my realities of myself. The reality that I had no idea how to support someone else emotionally and the simple fact that she would need a tremendous amount of space in the coming months to find inner healing from the things that got her here to Yakima. There were a lot of nights of frustration for me because I thought she was being selfish and playing games with me. Yeah Mark, I could really like you, the timing is not right. I'm not closing the door I just need to find my inner healing first. I need freedom from the bondage of my past and that's what she would tell me. Sure, lets be friends.

This had its ups and downs and It was difficult for me to slow down and start with my recovery. I had to get my focus off her and find restoration for the areas of my life that were broken that got me here. I had to essentially let her go in my mind, I had to learn to be friends, and I had to learn to allow her space. I had to learn the tools offered in recovery to abstain from drugs and alcohol. I had to face the reality that our lives were pretty messed up, and that we had a lot of work to do in all areas to become functioning members in society again.

It was very hard to keep this feeling I thought was love for her in perspective as just one of many things that needed to be repaired in my life. Repaired all the way back to the day I was abandoned at age two. Recovery that included learning to trust people again before I could ever understand what the four letters of love even meant. Yes, then there is the fact of not having a job, no license, no car, reckless driving warrant, pending bankruptcy, no development of coping skills except to gamble, spend recklessly, and drive fast or use drugs when my inner self felt insecure in this place called life.

However, she dominated so much of my thinking. The whole situation just had too many similarities of the love I already lost at age 18. The beautiful person that felt God said let me go to heal. Please God, could this be my healing, 13 years later? Please Lord, help me focus and take every area of my life in recovery so serious so I don't lose again. Really though, my forever underlying thought now, back to her, God, are you giving me a second chance to have love in my life? Don't let me lose her is what I'd pray. Don't let me falter in my journey and fall short of exposing every negative area of my own behavior to find inner healing and positive correction to that I can be a well-balanced and fully able to offer myself to her. Isn't it interesting the times you choose to pray to God?

Although we never started dating, she became one of my best friends in recovery. I shared so much of my inner pains with her; she gave me strength and support, and she gave me motivation and direction. I owe so much of my recovery to her. I owe so much of the words on these pages to her. But the beating drum of time must march forward and people must go down their own road in recovery. Although we are not as close as the beginning stages of recovery, she is in my thoughts and heart always and I miss her. She'll always remain in my heart as one of the best friends I could have. She is someone that will never be replaced in my heart by another.

So I'm left with the useless feeling that my life is one of those movies where people reach a crossroads in their lives and make the wrong decision. As the movie continues, you watch a person continue to live a life making one bad decision after another always trying to regain what they keep losing day after day. They are lost in the fact of what they no longer have anything that they used to value. Then at the end of the movie they wake up and realize it was all a bad dream and they still have everything. No time had past and it was all processed in their subconscious. However, upon awakening from their sleep they realized the potential effects of their bad decisions and were now equipped to take the other turn at the crossroads and make positive real life decisions as if the events had actually occurred. Real wisdom gained by the absent physical factor of time. I ponder on this thought; a lifetime where I am standing at another crossroads'. Unlike a movie, this is reality.

Now my daily routine includes 6:30 am early bird of the 12-step recovery program meetings, hangout with Abbey and her mother in the morning, meeting Rebekah for lunch, hanging out at a local coffee shop with Abbey working on our psychology assignments until Rebekah was off work and the three of us would go to the 6:30pm 12-step recovery meeting. Then we'd hang out at the pizza parlor or Abbey's house for dinner and a movie. This routine happened for about five weeks until I finally had a night of tears. God, what am I doing here? Please just let me go home as I cried with Rebekah at the pizza shop. She took me home and then she leaned in to kiss me. I didn't kiss her, I couldn't. I felt broken inside although I wanted to be with her, but I didn't feel adequate.

That night I go home and pray for help. As I close my eyes and lean back in my chair, I pray "God, I'm here, what am I doing?" I'm no longer working in my profession of almost nine years, I don't have a car or license anymore, I have a pending reckless driving incident, I've gambled away everything I own, forcing bankruptcy, and I've used all my friends and hanging on to any support my family is willing to give me. Why am I here? Why Rebekah? Why Abbey? Why these housemates? Why Yakima? Why am I alive? The song by Creed comes called with Arms Wide Open. Some of the lyrics say… "I just heard the news today it seems my life is going to change. I close my eyes and begin to pray as tears of joy stream down my face… I'll show you everything if you follow me with arms wide open…" I tell God, the one that I'm so blindly praying to as a choice of my program suggested higher power, "I'll follow." I get this visual of traveling through a dark corridor. As I lift my head from the chair with my eyes still closed, I see this bright light. In my minds eye, it is the light out of the darkness if I choose to enter, or leave for that matter. Perhaps the peacefulness of a blue sky is amidst a burning inferno. In reality it's the light from my bedroom light. This becomes a turning point in my recovery.

One afternoon Abbey and I went to have her nails done. It's on 40th avenue in Yakima in a shopping center by a coffee shop. The nail boutique is owned and operated by this really neat Vietnamese family. For whatever reason, and this is not my first visit to his shop, the owner starts a conversation with me about the Asian culture. This is weird because he does not talk much. He explains that baby's that are born out of wedlock are sold for profit. He explains if the baby is kept and not sold, the mother is ostracized from the family and cannot receive any government help at all. My first inclination is that I'm not excited about the conversation. However, I'm intrigued; I've never heard the words he is telling me. I process the conversation later and try to understand how it must have felt for my biological mother. How does it feel to have to choose between keeping your son and maintaining your position in your family, your bloodline? Having to choose between the life that you bore or being able to have a job and remain in the Korean culture?

I replay the scenario of what it must have been like for my biological family to be forced to give up their son. I feel pain, I feel hurt, I feel sadness, I feel grief, I feel anger, and I feel betrayed. I cry endless tears from the deepest parts of my feelings locked in my vault of abandonment. I accept a newfound respect for my mother, my father, my family, and my culture. I respect the sacrifices my mother made. She kept me hidden until I was too big to keep. I respect her choice to leave me in the safest place possible to ensure I was protected and able to have the chance to live. I respect the healing process and understand that I have turned another page, another page further from the dark chapters of my life.

Unbeknownst to me I begin traveling through a multitude of spiritual experiences. God reveals a number of painful areas in my life that I was unwilling before to look at let alone entertain the notion of letting go and allowing God to heal. The days become emotionally tougher. The nights become overwhelming to process everything. Night after night as I rest my head for sleep, I have another enlightening and defining moment in recovery. One spiritual experience after another, I cannot stop them. I embrace God's strength as I wake in tears feeling pain that engulfs my entire body. I can't continue, but I can't go back. I pray between gasps of air to walk me through my innermost pain. Reliving my trauma, heal my heart, my mind, my body, and spirit.

God opens another closed door in my vault of pain. This time in my dream I am with a woman that is helping me place this lifeless child on the top bunk of a bunk bed. The child's body is twisted and I needed to get a pillow for it to lay to rest. I left that house and crossed a paved area that was surrounded by a chain link fence. As I was walking up the wooden stairs I was walking with the woman in my dream. I wound around the next set of stairs into a gray rectangular two-story type house; It was old and with a long hallway. As I was going through I walk to the other side and then outside of the house. There were all these cars; I remember a red truck owned by someone hanging out ridiculing me. Then I looked around and realized everyone was ridiculing me. I went back into the house and there were all these kids on the second floor that weren't there before. I started racing through the long hallway and these kids were poking at me. They were chasing me, lashing out at me. Most of them were physically deformed, like they were in this house to be hidden from society. I ran down the stairs and slammed the outside door. The top half of it was bent and one of the worst deformed kids was pushing through the hole in the door where the door handle should be; this child had one eye. I slammed the door and ran back to the paved stairs in between the two houses where the woman was waiting for me. She was gone, just an empty shell remained. I opened her wallet that was on the ground and it was empty. I remember her taking three cards out of it and a bottle of what I thought was prescription pills. I was hurt because she was not there to help me. Then I suddenly remembered I forgot to get the pillow. I had to find it in myself to run back into the house. One of the deformed kids broke rank and helped me find a pillow. It was rectangle and flat, yellow, brownish color with four knobby things sewed on it. I ran back out and slammed the door shut for good, even the bent part at the top. I went back into the other house and placed the pillow under the lifeless child's head for comfort.

Like the empty shell in my dream, I understand it's also just as significant a reflection of me. I can't say I support if I don't have support to give. If people reach out in trust for me or anyone else for that matter that cannot be there in support. We have to find the strength within ourselves to face our own demons of our past. That realization is between God and me. But it's that same realization that God shows others that they can do this and when that happens. It's only then that when we realize once it is done we will possess the ability to support someone else because of what we have finally allowed ourselves to do. It's only then that we realize we've always possessed that ability. People cannot give what they don't have and they cannot receive what someone else cannot give. We have the ability to break these cycles.

That dream helped me understand that my healing process has to be from God and in him is where my strength should rest. God will not fail because he designed me and knows how to heal me. As people progress in the program of recovery, and when the time comes to share, support and let go, and trust in God. Only when people step aside to allow God to take us through the final passage of healing.

As another restless night continues, I awake from another dream that keeps me from solid sleep. In my dream, I'm trying to escape from a sinking ship, through the ill advice of old friends with scuba gear that didn't fit. I remember my feet hitting what I thought were two poles of some sort on the sinking ship as I swam. Then I woke up. I didn't put much thought into it until later in the day when I went to Moses Lake to ride in a speedboat and go tubing. What a rush hitting the wakes at 60mph. When I was there floating in the water I looked up and before my eyes saw the exact two towers that I thought were poles were hitting my feet in my dream from the sinking ship I was trying to escape. They were cellular towers. I saw a child in the reflections of the clouds in the water. I saw three angels surrounding it and heard kids laughing and playing in the background; It felt surreal. The laughter was real though; it was coming from one of the houses on the lake in the distant background. I smiled at the child in the clouds reflecting in the water. Who are you? Do I know you? Are you me? Are you my lost child? You're safe and happy now, aren't you?

Months later during the recovery process, I have a conversation with my mother that brings my baby dreams full circle. She tells me of my early days as a child. She tells me how I used to wake up screaming in the middle of the night and she couldn't wake me up. She would just hold me. Night, after night, after night I would say things in Korean. As I got older the nightmares were still there, but my words were in English. She said I would say mommy, daddy, baby, oh no! Suddenly I relive the painful dreams of me facing evils that lay to rest a dead child. Suddenly, I relive the memories of dreams of a child protected by angels. I cry on the phone as I begin to smile inside. I don't know what I saw as a child and I don't know where this goes, but it's freedom and I can feel healing on the horizon.

It was only later in recovery that I learned that to understand where most of the suffering alcoholics are at emotionally and intellectually. This path of exposure and healing is not for everyone, especially for the already emotionally battered. As they choose, It's important for them to have a support network. Otherwise, with a past like many, what else would they have? Most have lost all their family members. Outside of the halls of the 12-step recovery program meetings, nobody cares if the stay sober or get drunk. What a blessing for me that my family cares. I had to learn to let the advice from others roll off and not get caught in the trap of verbal debates with others. It's a very healthy reflection to look back at. My personal feel is that's the start of healthy living, learning to not take ownership of other peoples opinions, and to respect why it's important too them versus trying to change their mind. Also helps to find use and purpose for their lives. It's also important as I resume life to learn how to develop new behaviors and life skills. The behaviors I used to practice were in place to protect certain painful areas of my life. As these areas are addressed I'm completely learning new ways to deal with every situation and scenario possible.

So after about five weeks without a sponsor, I finally found one who had all these requirements that I thought I needed. Someone that is stern, doesn't sugar coat things, confident, goal orientated, long-term sobriety, knowledgeable of the big book yet open to understanding other areas of life that may need to be addressed that may or may not be described in the book (i.e., cognitive behavioral therapy). I also wanted someone that was balancing a family and educated and self-reliant.

I found these qualities in someone and his name is Ricky. He's spent 3 ½ years in prison and his drug of choice is heroin. He knows the 12-step recovery book almost verbatim. He doesn't tell me what to do, rather, if I have a question, he'll tell me what he did and say the knowledge is for me to make a decision with. He recognizes what worked for him may not work for me. He balances a family and works as a therapist for Behavioral Health Services. He has his Chemical Dependency Certificate and Masters Degree in Psychology. The Governor also expunged his record several years ago restoring his right to be a productive member of society. After almost ten years of sobriety Ricky still attends daily 12-step recovery program meetings, sponsors people like myself, does speaker events at the 12-step recovery program functions and other treatment facilities. He leads a life by example of the progression of his own. His closing words to me are always, "Mark, don't drink, don't use, and how willing do you need to be? As willing as the dying can be!" He is a man that is teaching me to stand on my own two feet. A man who'll never know the impact he has in saving my life from the destruction of the disease that I live. He is a man that is from God for a purpose on earth today; a purpose to save lives. Thank you Ricky from the bottom of my heart.

On August 17, 2004 I start my first day of employment at Sundown M Ranch. It was actually only during my employment that I really understood the wide range of treatment services available for chemically addicted persons. So what type of services is available one might ask? There are outpatient, inpatient and psychiatric hospitals as follows:

Outpatient – Intensive outpatient does not require the patient to sleep at the facility and is divided into three phases:

1. Phase I – Meets three to four days a week for two to three hours and requires written proof of weekly 12-step recovery program attendance. Groups consist of education about alcohol and drugs and their adverse effects. Approximate length is three months.

2. Phase II – Weekly group check-ins facilitated by a counselor and last an hour and a half to two hours. Approximate length is six months.

3. Phase III – Monthly group check-ins facilitated by a counselor and last an hour and a half to two hours. Approximate length is nine months.

Inpatient – Treatment requires round the clock stay at an inpatient or residential treatment facility. Length of time is dependant on the type of service needed. Services are divided into three levels of care:

1. Level I - Lowest level of care is more or less residential chemical dependency treatment. These programs are voluntary and are approximately 21 – 28 days in continuous over night stay.

2. Level II – Generally have medical doctors on staff and treat patients that have advanced from a lower level of care.

3. Level III – Secure facilities that have alarms on the doors and windows. Generally have medical doctors and administer detoxification medications.

Psychiatric Hospitals – Longer term lock down facilities.

1. Psychiatric Hospital – Lockdown facility where chemical dependency and other co-existing disorders like manic depression, opposition defiance disorder, attention deficit hyperactive disorder are treated simultaneously. Psychiatric analysis is performed, medications administered and the length of stay dependant on rehabilitation.

So what is Sundown M Ranch? It is a level I residential inpatient chemical dependency treatment facility. It is the lowest level of chemical dependency inpatient treatment that the State of Washington allows. They do not have psychiatric staff or 24-hour medical doctors or nursing staff. They do not prescribe medications nor detox people from their chemical use. They do not have security guards and it is not a lock down facility. Rather, it's a voluntary, around the clock, a 21-day program for adults and 28 days for youth.

So what does my typical workday include? On Tuesday, Wednesday and Thursday I work as an admission specialist. I receive a range of callers from individuals wanting help for their drug and alcohol use, concerned family members seeking help for their loved ones, probation officers, counselors, interventionist and the occasional suicide call. We try to get an overview of the persons mental, physical and emotional history, including any medications, criminal background, to determine whether Sundown M Ranch is the right level of care or if they need something we cannot offer, like a psychiatrist or medications for a coexisting disorder.

What happens behind the scenes is the battle with the insurance companies. As I have come to realize today, the power of the disease of alcoholism, is a disease that will take daily work and for many people, several attempts at treatment. However, that is not the same view shared by the insurance industry. Most have provisions for one or two treatments in a two-year span. That creates the misconception that in 21-days you can be cured from your alcoholism. I'm not so sure where the communication has been broken. If it is in fact a disease then there maybe continual follow-up to keep it in remission. I would think that could mean lifelong follow-up that may include multiple treatments. If it's not a disease and it can be cured with one or two treatments, than I don't understand the classification by the medical and insurance professionals. I would hope it's not simply for payment sake at the expense of people's lives.

I have come to realize how hard it is to get a loved one through treatment because of the differing views between the medical professionals treating this as a lifelong chronic and progressive disease versus the insurance industry that only provides a very limited amount of coverage that implicitly implies a one shot deal and your cured. Hmmmmm.

Then, on Friday and Saturday, I process the new patients; more or less being the first face they will see when they arrive to Sundown M Ranch. I explain their schedule for the next 21 days, and try to keep them at ease, while answering questions, as they sign their paperwork and start the next chapter of their life. My new employment in a nutshell.

Although not fully written, there are a lot of tears that were shed over many personal losses that are not in these pages. I pray that you find the strength to continue and allow God to take you through the same healing tears in your own life.

XV

Reconstruction of a Broken Life

As I recap the events of my life, I slowly understand what recovery is all about. The alcohol, drugs, gambling, sex, all the self-destructive behaviors are packaged into one thing. The greatest distraction to keep me from internal healing and true usefulness in this journey called life.

Recovery for me, as it began with the 21-day chemical dependency treatment at Sundown M Ranch, progressed to clean and sober living, cognitive behavioral therapy and spiritual cleansing, a point that most people stop, but by far the most rewarding. From the very beginning of recovery, I had to abandon everything I thought I knew at this point in life. I had to become willing to rid myself, at least temporarily, of the thought that my thinking and decision making skills that I have developed up to this point in life were reasonable. Since Sundown M Ranch is not a dual diagnosis facility. They do not have psychiatrists or psychologists and they do not prescribe medications for ailments like depression, anxiety, etc. Sundown M Ranch utilizes individuals that have dealt with past alcohol and chemical dependency addictions and have since been certified by the State of Washington as a Certified Chemical Dependency counselors. They promote the belief is that we are born with the disease of alcoholism that has chemically altered our genealogy and makes it impossible too make healthy, productive life decisions on our own. Our chemical makeup is designed to protect areas of pain in our life. As we progress we develop reactionary behaviors to protect those areas of pain from being exposed and making us vulnerable to the rest of the world. If we use alcohol or drugs, the areas of pain we are protecting become un-manageable and our reactionary behaviors become more forthright and aggressive. More use, more aggression, more aggression, more use. Why? We still have feelings and our aggression makes us feel bad. Therefore, the intake of a mind or mood altering substance allows us to live without a conscious for the actions and lives we are leading. Until the drugs wear off.

As this vicious cycle continues, at one point the chemical makeup becomes so altered, to a point that it may appear to have created permanent changes and in-ability to make any personal decisions on our own. Everything becomes un-manageable. Every decision is overwhelming.

The concept of Sundown M Ranch is to break the vicious cycle by promoting complete abstinence from any mind or mood altering substance. If the person can abstain from drugs and alcohol long enough, the clouded thinking can be made clear and a point of manageability within our lives can be obtained. This can only be obtained if we understand that we cannot do things alone. We need to become willing to rid ourselves of all negative and destructive thinking by way of cleansing ourselves internally of the areas of pain that we have become so accustomed to protecting. This is done by working the 12 steps of a 12-step-recovery-program. At Sundown M Ranch the treatment is focused on the first five steps:

1. We admitted we were powerless over alcohol - that our lives had become unmanageable.

2. Came to believe that a power greater than ourselves could restore us to sanity.

3. Made a decision to turn our will and our lives over to the care of God as we understood him.

4.   Made a searching and fearless moral inventory of ourselves.

5.   Admitted to God, to ourselves, and to another human being the exact nature of our wrongs.

During the group counseling we worked intensely with these steps. We completed internal inventories of ourselves to include every person we've hurt and taken advantage of, the things we've stolen or used without permission, and an inventory of all the substances and drugs we've ever used. We also shared as many of the things done to us that we are in pain over like family deaths, physical, verbal or sexual abuse, significant mental, physical and/or emotional losses. We also looked at our many negative feelings of self and started to develop ways to replace these with positive character attributes.

But when did these negative feelings of self begin? If you believe in the disease concept of alcoholism, then it started at birth. The inception of time that the world began to lie to me and I started to believe that I was un-worthy and accepted all the negative associations that go with those. My abandonment, parent's divorce, death, and self-destruction confirmed the lies in my head. We have to expose and let go of our sources of pain in order to move forward, ultimately accepting the fact that I am a good person and believing it. We feel tears of healing pain as we let go of a false belief system.

I'm a worthy person. I'm loveable, deserving, selfless, happy, witty, smart, kind, generous, giving, witty, intelligent, humorous, intuitive, leader, strong, driven, focused, trusting. These values God created me with. When I entered the world I believed lies and started living and making choices based on lies. Lies that told me I was worthless, un-trustworthy, un-loveable, un-kind, malicious, hurtful, reckless, lost, alone, un-trustworthy, un-deserving. As I aged in life I experienced a number of occasions that fed the lie. I looked for anything to medicate the pain. What was the pain? It was pain stemming from the belief that I was all these lies. What a piece of garbage I must be. But how? There was always a piece of hope in me, I just didn't know what it was. I do today.

It was my original value system and character that God gave me that was fighting against my belief of all the lies that I accepted as me. A game of internal tug of war. As I progressed through life and made decisions based on the false belief that I was worthless it helped me develop self-defeating behaviors that continually fed the lie. It's not true. Then in comes emotional pain. Why, because I'm stuffing the fact that the decisions I'm making are not congruent with the value system God gave me. This would cause tremendous pain, because then I would have to accept that I was living a lie. I medicated this pain in many fashions. I found ways to take me away temporarily, so that I would not have to think of these conflicting feelings inside.

I believe we are all created this way. We're alcoholics and a simple DUI can bring us into chemical dependency treatment to learn the 12-steps of recovery and healthy living, in terms that we may not consciously have ever thought of before. Other 12-step based groups include gambling, over-eating, sex, but very few of those are utilized because they are not in result of direct legal recourse from the court system that requires participation in a 12-step based recovery program. We're very lucky, at least the ones that can avoid the dismal negativity and continual drug use and thieving from the personalities of the others that don't want to be here. Ones that are simply thrown here by the legal system. If we work the principles of the 12-steps, we are very lucky. We finally get too accept and use the values God gave us. Today, my decisions are matched against my value system. Do they compliment?

However, this discovery does not remove all the pain of hurting others and ourselves. Again, where does the hurt stem from? We lashed out at others. Why? Parent's divorce, death, etc., Not true. Those may be contributing factors to the source of internal pains. These are external situations that allow us to believe a false reality of our selves. We're un-worthy. Why else would I have lost my child? I don't deserve good things! But I do, that was the little spark of hope that kept me alive. I knew for too many years that life was not as it appeared. I just couldn't find answers. It's all lies! The world is designed to take the God given gifts you posses, feed you lies, and watch you destroy yourself, so you never have the opportunity to expose the truth to anybody else.

You cannot give what you don't posses. What you don't posses is acceptance of the fact that God already gave you the gifts. Accept them. Stop the vicious search for answers of all the external unknowns; it will only keep you chasing your tail, creating turmoil and doubt. You owe it to yourself and to me to accept the God given gifts already within you and stop living based on a lie.

This enlightenment is very powerful for me. I feel so much more confident about myself and my abilities. It's like it's a natural fit. Why? Because it is. Even using them the first day seems like they were never lost. It's not learning a new belief system, it's accepting and using the one I already have, which is 180 degrees opposite of the one I've used my entire life.

I could go for one hundred years searching for closure and healing on all the external havoc that I created in an attempt to believe my false beliefs of me. It's a never-ending search. But that's not what it's all about. It's accepting who I am. The external things take care of themselves, in God's timing. Why, because I'm no longer living life based on those scenarios. I'm living life based on my original value system and those old external scenarios no longer control my life. It's not about hurrying up to find the answers so I can get on with life. It's about hurrying up to accept me, so that in God's timing I'm prepared to close those chapters when the time is right, never letting them hold me back from moving forward again.

The ultimate goal of the chemical dependency counselors is that we are released from our inner pain and false negative beliefs are replaced with positive character assets. We would no longer need to drink or use drugs to suppress our feelings, good or bad. We could then start to change our behaviors to include positive and healthy lifestyle choices that don't include alcohol or drug use. However, this will take a lifetime of breaking old behaviors and adopting new ones. The sad part is that most people in recovery don't make it this far, 90% relapse and never get past the initial treatment phase, which is just trying to keep them off drugs and alcohol.

Another phase of my recovery was when I was recommended to relocate Yakima, Washington and stay in an Oxford home, or shared recovery house, with other recovering alcoholics, until completion of the 90-day weekly outpatient with Sundown M Ranch. I was also referred to a local psychologist for cognitive behavioral therapy to treat my compulsive gambling. My initial diagnosis was off the chart as a martyr with a recommendation for a mild anti-depressant and anti-anxiety medication. My psychologist and I agreed to postpone the medications to allow the effects from abstaining from drugs and alcohol to take affect and the development of new behaviors. If those disorders still exist after 90-days then we would revisit the possibility of medications. Today I don't take those prescription medications.

My psychological appointments included completion of an autobiography to identify areas of hurt. We spent a majority of the time at my abandonment. Working through areas of pain and developing new ways to cope with those feelings I have suppressed for so very long. Understanding I no longer need to react to life the way I have for so many years. Once the feelings are recognized and an understanding of who I really am is gained, a whole lifestyle of new choices need to be developed and practiced. This part can take a lifetime and is often where many people revert to old behaviors. They've not completely abandoned old characteristics, let go of pain, or accepted things are not there fault, and that they are a good and worthy person. Sometimes life circumstances arise causing a relapse of old behaviors leading ultimately back to continued substance use to once again hide the negative pain. Although the pain and hurts may be gone, it may take a lifetime to redevelop new behaviors and decision-making capacities. We don't need our old behaviors anymore. However, this is for me and me alone to understand about my recovery and myself. Otherwise it's very easy to become judgmental.

To blame the disease solely, is to forego responsibility for our actions. I agree that people who have the mental and emotional capacity to make healthy decisions don't need to fall on the crutch of the disease concept forever, only for a short time to uncloud their thinking and allow them time to make tough, positive decisions. The trap is that most of our lives have been destroyed internally and externally during our using days. Getting sober means the roller coaster stops and we now get to clean up all our wreckage, which includes for many people incarceration for past crimes. This is the point a lot of people say, why? The point needs to be made that freedom from past life is such a hard earned reward if we work for it.

Some people are fortunate enough to rebound fairly quickly from the wreckage of their past, these people are few and far between the masses that become chemically dependant for any great length of time. Most of the people in recovery have altered their brain chemistry so badly that they have become borderline, if not completely, mentally ill. They don't have the luxury or emotionally stability to process decisions like the preceding paragraph. The steps they are taking today are the gateway between living a life in society, having a sponsor make decisions for you, or medications in a mental facility. I don't know if they have the capacity to understand their role in their negative behaviors without making them feel so horrible and causing them to use. Almost healthier that they not question the disease factor, keep going to meetings and never fully accept responsibility for what they are doing and rely 100% on a sponsor to keep them sober and influence every aspect of their lives. There is another way. Only God can remove the mental illness that lies within the altered brain chemistry. Only God can heal your past pains, just like he has mine in the areas I've so vaguely described. I hope it inspires you to seek your own God of understanding and healing so that you may share in the freedom of self that I have been given today.

I think my big recovery hurdle came when I was forced to accept responsibility for my decisions in life. Forced to begin the process of cleaning up the wreckage of my past. This clean up included bankruptcy, court for a reckless driving warrant, and employment at really the only place that would work with a guy with a suspended license and no vehicle. Doing the hard part to make inner stability and embrace the consequences for my actions. The 12-Step Recovery Program meetings and psychologist really helped me understand that I have low self-worth. Accepting that fact and understanding ways to counter its effects. Rather than a series of small negative behaviors that result in large consequences or chaos. The way to prevent the large negative consequences is to minimize that amount of small negative behaviors. This removes pain, how do you go on the other side? We do a series of small positive behaviors that compound and produce a large happy consequence. Now I have reached normalism. Development of coping skills. Perhaps a continual 10th step? Who knows. I do know that I am the type of person that has to consciously put effort into working on a daily series of small positive decisions. Otherwise, I will too easily fall back into the world I was previously in.

Education, changing behaviors, accepting myself, understanding the chemical makeup of my body, processing feelings and emotions, and a daily fight to not drink alcohol or use drugs is a great start for me. These are all things that can be managed within myself. However, as I understand and accept the disease of alcoholism that I have, these positive changes will ultimately make me miserable. Why? My body is hard wired differently than other people. It does not produce a stabilizing amount of chemicals from my brain that enables me to not feel hopeless, with an underlying thought of unworthiness. Illicit drugs release the dopamine that stabilizes my body to a level that the rest of society takes for granite. This is why abstinence is the ultimate setup for relapse. It has to become more. It has to become a complete physical, emotional, mental and spiritual metamorphous. The body needs new wiring.

There is another level that goes so deep within my soul, a side of inner healing that changes the way I think of myself and view the entire world. A level that allows me to trust and love, a spiritual side that breaks the lies of my past and reconstructs a new beginning, with the help of a power greater than myself. This deeper level reaches a very personable place associated with my abandonment, that I reacted in so many self-destructive ways, my entire life. Four areas of spiritual enlightenment and healing for me to break the vicious cycle have been:

1. Physical Security- As a child being abandoned before the age of two and a half, I had my physical and emotional security taken away. Life has thrown other things in my direction that have reinforced that if I don't take I won't have. The lack of physical security makes me feel helpless, like the elements could kill me and there are no walls, let alone people to protect me. My defense to that is to have a bigger and better four walls, to never get hurt, like my armor against life. Unfortunately, these walls (homes, cars, money, people, etc.,) were gained at the expense of others. I obtained what was desired by others to keep me in their graces and protection. But that is a farce. When I take things form other people that do not belong to me, it compromises the protection that others have built for themselves, which causes them to feel un-safe and in fear of their own physical security. Aren't we all in search of the same thing? When these protections are removed

or in danger I react in fear and ultimately take more. True understanding comes when knowing that God is my protector and provider and I don't need more. Despite the beliefs of the world, God is to be shared with others in hopes they can find this protection as well.

2. Emotional Security- In the Korean culture a baby born out of wedlock places the mom in great danger. She has two choices. Either give up for adoption too maintain her place in her family and society. Or keep the child and become ostracized from her family, losing her family name and rights and removed from the culture losing her chance for employment and government assistance in any way. God has shown me that being kept alive for my first two and a half years meant a lot of hiding in sometimes un-safe, physical conditions, and also being constantly told to be quiet in fear of being exposed, which at any age after birth could have led to death in fear of being caught. What I interpreted was that if I cried or longed for my mother's emotional security and protection, it would be my fault if she lost hers. Today as I learn to communicate and reach out for help, it breaks my false belief that when I cry for help, it won't cause somebody else to lose his or her life, rather, it will save mine.

3. Approval of Others- Because I was ultimately abandoned, I have always felt I wasn't good enough. I felt that things were my fault that I could not stay in my own family and culture. I've lived my whole life trying to earn my spot and not be abandoned by another family or culture. In result I've tried so hard to please others never wanting to be a disappointment out of fear that they would abandon me. Disapproval from others is translated in my mind as failing them, and therefore I would be abandoned, which means compromising physical and emotional security, ultimately leading to real life fear of death. God is revealing to me that I don't need to have the approval of others to ward off death. The only approval I need is from him and to strive to live a life that improves the life that happens after I leave here, not to be in such protection of my temporary existence on Earth. I can live without fear today knowing that as I leave this earth I know where I'm going.

4. Protector- I had a dream of my mother's second husband. I was on a yacht (representing material armor) and he called for me. I answered the phone and he asked about the political fundraising I am doing for my father (representing money as an armor). Then he asked if the others were around. Both Sherri and Dana were telling me no, they did not want to talk to him. Then somebody mentioned Dana's name in the background and Frank flipped out on the phone (representing my emotional armor). He started yelling telling me how could I lie to him and tell them the ones he wanted to talk to weren't around. Then he implied he would not give towards the campaign, which attacked my financial armor that would lead to compromising my physical armor leaving me more vulnerable and susceptible to death.

When I woke up God showed me something. He reinforced that he is my armor and protector; I don't need these false armors to stay alive. He also told me that it wasn't my fault. After the divorce I assumed in my level of feelings a responsibility as the father figure or protector to my siblings. In that dream I felt like I failed them because I could not protect them from him. I also felt like it was my fault if anything bad ever happened to them. This is a very vicious cycle. It's not my fault. These feelings of failure and fault that I've lived an entire life feeling are rooted so far in my vault of abandonment. If someone ever showed displeasure with me, it meant throwing me in harms way, just like being silenced as a child in fear of being discovered for being a life that wasn't supposed to live. Feelings of inadequacy and fear that ultimately make me feel the helpless, abandoned child.

Knowing what I have learned about myself, it's important for me to maintain a balanced life and to keep the forward progression going, well... forward. Not too much 12-step recovery programs, not too much work, not too much inter-personal relationships, not too much psychologist appointments, not too much volunteer effort, not too much adoption support groups and not too much alone time. A healthy balance between work, play and self-help in many different categories for my life.

Today my life includes employment at Sundown M Ranch in the admission department, weekly 12-step recovery program meetings, and on-going development of interpersonal relationships beginning with my sponsor. I am also a guest lecturer at Sundown M Ranch and James Oldham Treatment Center, drunk driving victim panels, and Yakima Valley Barrios Unidos, anti gang and community mobilization efforts. I share my life story and what recovery has done for me, in hope to provide inspiration to someone else that the road less traveled has rewards. I also attend monthly adoption support groups to address the underlying issues dealing with abandonment, the very cause of my childhood trauma that I spent a lifetime of hurting people, self medicating through drugs, alcohol, gambling, crime and hurting so many people through my misplaced anger. Furthermore, I continue developing my spiritual life and gaining a new understanding of who God is to me. This is just the beginning of my healing process.

My final thoughts as I venture off into the rest of my life are neat reflections of stuff from my childhood. Old photos, report cards, and my clothes I came to America in. I was reading a newspaper article from January 1979 that my mother had given me. My dad was testifying in front of the house judiciary about house bill 4, which is a law passed after me. It was passed to allow foreign born adopted kids to receive Washington state birth certificates. In the picture I am sitting next to my dad. When they asked me if I have anything to add apparently I say that I'm 6-years old. Then in quotes "Brad Owen is my daddy". Isn't that cute? The age of innocence. Then of course I think to myself, what happened? When did I lose that innocence to life? To run and laugh and think so highly of those around me? When did I become so jaded? Then I think I know why recovery is so neat, it's my return to the age of innocence.

I close this chapter with a prayer to my family. My mother Nancy and her husband Terry. My father Brad and step mother Linda. My sisters Shanie, Dana and Sherri. My brother's Royce and Adam. I thank you for rescuing me from the probable death that my life was sure to face in the streets and orphanages of Korea. I'm sorry that I was so angry inside and chose to hurt each and everyone of you, by attempting to destroy anything that was important between us in our lives. I'm sorry and ask for your forgiveness. I thank you for loving me and pray that you will stand with me as I am sure to continually face feelings associated with my abandonment. I pray that we all understand that trauma changes life. Victory over these will require adoption of a whole new life, behaviors and coping mechanisms. At 32-years old, I have a lifetime of new behaviors to learn, develop and practice. As my pains are being healed there is a learning curve of time to develop new behaviors, as I will no longer need my old guards and defenses. I pray that you understand that like an onion, the healing process may be just that, a lifetime of peeling my internal onion. I know today that this will happen in waves, as my heart is ready, just like yours.

XVI

Bleeding Family Hearts

Dear Mark;

    Basically, you were a very easy child to raise. Oh, you had your moments, but over all you were very easy. I enjoyed being your mother very much! In fact, I LOVED being your mother! I am awed at what a blessed woman I have been to be allowed by God to be the one to raise you! I have always been so proud of you. You are very intelligent, even brilliant, you have a great sense of humor, you are fun to be with, and you have a compassionate and kind heart. You have a wonderful heart, but it seemed, as you got older that you were trying to run away from whom you were inside. I remember when an evangelist once spoke a prophetic word over you and said you had a heart like David. I knew that always!! David was kind and compassionate, but also he was very courageous, and above all he trusted God and didn't care what others thought about his love for the Lord. He had failings, but always came back to his first love, the Lord. He was passionate about the Lord! He knew God and he wanted to make Him known to his people.

When you kids were little I took you to every Walt Disney and kids movie that came out in the theater. Even when I had to work, I tried to give you my weekends with a movie and dinner at a burger or pizza restaurant. I'm so sad you don't you remember those times. I know I took you kids alone, but you always had fun. You had both of us at your birthdays until 1980. Of course that would have made you only eight years old. I sometimes had two parties for you, one for family, which both of us would be at, and one with neighbor kids, which usually I was the one with you.

Babysitters were when you were younger and Brad and I were still married. During this time I had to work in our convenient stores, not after we moved to Harvard street house, nor after the divorce. I was finally able to be home with my children!!! It was a dream of finally being a mother!

When we moved to Hawaii, I was not there to rely on YWAM for survival Mark. I was there because the Lord told me too go there. I worked to stay there and provide for us. YWAM never forced anything upon anyone. We were there because of our belief and YWAM provided an avenue to fulfill those desires. The government housing we lived in was not substandard per the State of Hawaii. The State of Hawaii only qualified us for state medical aid because Adam needed medical attention for his ears. The caseworker informed me that we qualified for food stamps along with the medical assistance. I only used the food stamps twice. Once for a three-month period and once for a two month period. Mark, isn't it interesting that we never missed a meal? I admit that some of the meals might not be what we wanted, but there was never a missed meal. God always provided for us.

There were times while you kids were growing up that I didn't know how we would survive, or where our next meal would come from! I was a wife beaten, betrayed and emotionally, physically and financially drained, but my life and my passion were to raise you kids to the best of my ability. I know what it is like to want to end your life, I've been there. But it was raising you kids that kept me going. We had to live through the choices that others made that affected us.

There were times I'd be so overwhelmed in the middle of the night I'd get up and literally lay face down with my arm out in front of me on the kitchen floor crying out to God for help! I did not know how I'd pay the rent or how we'd survive. By God's grace we always made it through. We cannot control what others do to us. Life comes at us, but it's what we do with it that counts. I put my hope in the Lord he is healing the past so that my future is released to it's fullest. My prayer is that all my children will receive the same healing touch from the Lord. He is the same yesterday, today, and forever. He can go back in time, He created time. Where the lies of rejection and worthlessness were embedded in our minds He can come in and reveal what is really true! He is renewing my mind and healing my heart and my prayer is that He you will all receive that same renewing and healing.

I love you to pieces!!!!!

Love,

Mom

The Life and Times of Mark Owen
Remarks by his dad, Brad Owen

When I first received the picture of Mark looking sad and alone at three years old in Korea I was immediately touched and excited about having a son in the family and giving this incredibly cute little boy a home. As many fathers I had envisioned going fishing, playing football and watching sports on TV together. It all started out just fine. The girls were great with him and he brought us all many days of fun and affection.

Some of the things that have stuck in my mind are relative to his adapting to a new environment. He did not speak English so communicating was difficult at times. At night he would wake up screaming and it would be impossible to know what the problem was although with his tough beginnings one could imagine. I would pick him up during these bouts and he would literally throw his head backwards bending his body until his head would touch his behind. It was frightening, but moving at the same time as I tried to comfort him because I knew he was entering a much better and safer life. It wasn't long until he just blended in with the rest of the family.

Watching Mark grow was a pleasant experience because he was so kind and likeable and never caused any trouble. Everybody was impressed by him. I knew, for that matter, I believe that everyone knew he would become a very successful young man with his own family. And then he turned.

It was one of the most disappointing points in my life to see this incredibly friendly, positive young man become a selfish person that acted as though he wanted nothing to do with the family. It was when he moved back to Washington from Hawaii and moved in with Linda and me. He would ignore rules and requests that we would make of him. I am sure that the "experts" would say that he was exercising his independence and stretching his wings. I can understand that, but it was not necessary to insult your family and change your personality to do that. Mark did.

I understand that it was when he first got in with some folks in Shelton that, as he put it to me one night, were going to be the Shelton mafia. One in particular was just an overblown, big shot that used young impressionable teens like Mark to do his dirty work. For some reason Mark saw this individual as "pretty cool". As Mark told me one night almost in awe of him, "he had never lost a fight". This was an indication of how Mark could be impressed and easily led into trouble in the future. It was a point when I saw all of the son that I had hoped and dreamed of and looked forward to being best friends with just disintegrate. Over the next several years it did not get better, it got worse.

There were some low points. It is very difficult to believe that your son could actually steal from you. When Mark did either through our store, or by filling out credit cards in Linda's name and nearly destroying her credit, I would not only be furious with him, but at other times find myself alone sitting, depressed and constantly wondering what happened, where is the Mark that we knew and the one we believed we would have as a son? Linda always bent over backwards to be a good mother to "my" kids and yet I would have to see her in tears because of the embarrassment she would go through every time we went in to the bank for a loan. He nearly destroyed her credit. We still have to deal with the impact of his actions to this day.

Mark took advantage of Adam wanting to be the good brother by helping Mark get a bank account that he could no longer get on his own. Adam was furious and incredibly hurt. His reputation with the bank was destroyed as Mark put him thousand's of dollars in debt and sending him to collections. All because his brother wanted to help him out.

Although I did not know for sure what Mark was using, I had a pretty good idea he and his "friends" were heavily into drugs. I thought many times of ways I could use some of my law enforcement contacts to put together a sting and nail them all. The purpose was to force him into the reality of where he was going and try to end it.

The most painful part of Mark's actions was how he impacted the rest of the family. I mentioned the effect it had on Linda, but there were his sisters and brothers and nieces and nephews. Of course Mark actions led him to prison. I took his sisters and nieces to visit him in prison in Idaho. I will never do that again. I will resist ever allowing my grandchildren to have to go through and see their parents and myself go through the indignity of visiting in a prison again.

I mention these situations with the family members because I am the dad. I am supposed to be able to fix things when they go wrong, help family members when they have troubles, make things better. With Mark I tried, I stepped in to help him in the early days with the court, give him a place to go when he said he wanted to turn things around or when the court said he had to have a place to go. Provide transportation, a car, help with school, and connections with jobs. I even got the family to do an intervention. Time and again, with Linda's support, I stepped up to help him. And then it was time to quit; to say no more, to realize he had to turn his life around on his own or crash. Linda and I agreed we had to be done and it was no longer our responsibility. Any further assistance would only be enabling him because he had become an expert at using and abusing everybody that did anything for him.

The difficulty with this decision was what I knew the consequences would be. It was so emotional that when I went to share this with Mark years later over the phone while Mark was preparing to go to Sundown M Ranch for treatment, I could not keep from crying out loud. I knew that I would eventually get a call that he was arrested and was going to prison or he was dead. But there was no other choice. It was the right choice. Mark crashed and lost everything he had left, which in reality was just his job and any reputation that he thought he had with his colleagues at work.

At this point I have great hope. It is hope admittedly with reservations because I have been there so many times before and been not only disappointed, but also kicked in the face. It is not to be unsupportive of Mark. I am completely supportive and am very proud of what he has done thus far, where he is, and what he is doing to give himself a new life. But, after twelve to fifteen years of lies, slams, insults and broken commitments, I cannot just accept everything is fixed and everyone will live happily ever after. What I know is that Mark has all of the ability in the world to stay clean and sober and accomplish great things. What will help us all is when he shows us a year, five years from now, and for the rest of his life that he is the man, the brother, the uncle and the son we all had hoped for, wanted so much and saw in him from the day we saw his picture from Korea.

Mark, make amends to the people you have wronged over the years and help others avoid the path that you took. That will make me very proud of you because it will show everyone what we all know you are; a good, caring person.

Mark, I love you very much and you are forgiven. I am very much looking forward to having the son, the best friend I saw in you so many years ago.

Dad

Dear Mark,

I cannot tell you how proud I am of how you have finally taken control over your addictions and your life!

Your first request was for forgiveness and my answer is YES, of course I do!! I believe a human being's capacity for love and forgiveness are two of God's greatest gifts to us.

Your second request for me write to you about the highs and lows of what is was like raising you is slightly overwhelming in that it has been so many years, so some of my comments will be pretty general and some specific. I think some things just fade over the years or perhaps I've chosen to let them fade for my own peace of mind.

It doesn't matter whether a person is a biological parent, adoptive parent or stepparent, (notice the key word "parent") we love all our children and always want what is best for them. Even though you did things I hated, I always loved you.

From the time I met you I loved you, but as you said in your writings, I didn't know you very well and all of a sudden I had an instant "other" family. I did know how I wanted to feel about you, and I did know I wanted to do the best I could at being a step mom. I knew I had an awesome responsibility, but I loved your dad so much I knew I was up for it. It took time for all of us to make adjustments to our new lives.

Unfortunately, because of your being moved to Hawaii, we only had the opportunity to contribute to your upbringing a couple of months every summer. It was difficult to make any significant impact on you in such a short period of time, but we forged ahead the best we could (even without the instruction manual on "How to Raise Children"). I don't know that you will completely understand (until you have children of your own), what it is like making the day to day decisions that influence the growth and development of your kids. I know that I did the best job I could under the circumstances, and then crossed my fingers as I anticipated the outcomes. I truly believe that all parents do that very same thing. However, when the best that you do supposedly goes awry, for whatever reason, it is counter productive to sit back and think that it could have been something you did or didn't do as a parent. My best intention was always, and will always be, to raise and influence all of you to the best of my abilities. I do not believe that the paths you chose had anything to do with the way you were raised.

When you were young and as you grew older, I remember having conversations with your dad about how we didn't need to worry about you getting involved in any negative behavior. You were so kind, gentle, loving, intelligent, funny, generous and giving. You were, and are good looking too, but I know that doesn't figure into the equation (or does it? Ha Ha). Of all our kids, you had a sense of direction and seemed to be heading in a certain direction. We just didn't realize it would be to all the wrong places! I remember being completely shocked by your behavior when you moved back here from Hawaii. You were so different. I wondered what those Hawaiians did to you that turned you into this person who wasn't Mark.

You had morphed into a very "difficult teenager." I remember feeling that "this too shall pass" as with most teenage behavior does. So I didn't really feel too concerned at that point. As time progressed it became very clear that there were bigger problems facing us. I remember feeling so sad and disappointed by this personality change. I longed for the loving boy you used to be to return. The next 10 – 12 years were the most challenging for me personally. You had done some incredibly stupid, insensitive and downright mean and cruel things to me, and too your dad. I couldn't understand how you could repay us for all the help, both emotionally and financially, we had given you. It didn't motivate me to seek any counseling, with or without you; it just plain pissed me off. After the anger subsided, there was always hope. Hope was the most recurring emotion I had in regard to you and your yet to be lived life. I never gave up hope that someday you would "see the light", and move on, in the direction that everybody who has ever know you, were convinced you would take.

As each of your setbacks occurred, I remember feeling deep sadness and was clearly frustrated over the "latest bad decision". But I also remember thinking that you would learn from this (finally), and hope would replace all the bad feelings once again. I mean, after all, you said you were sorry and learned from the mistake, and you would never do it again. You knew what you had to do, blah blah blah. The hardest part for us was that you were over 18 and legally an adult, so we couldn't force you to do anything. And I wanted to do plenty, trust me!

I know in your heart you already know this, but I wanted to put it down on paper, because I hope it will be more real to you that way. I have never, and will never give up on you, or any of my kids. I will always love you no matter what happens. I know that you weren't born to me, and I didn't formally adopt you, but I love you as if it were so. You are an incredibly fortunate person to have been given the opportunities you have, and continue to get, and it fills me with happiness to see you are resolving long standing issues, working through them, and finding your well deserved place in this world. I hope that in this process, you will find what you need with a minimal amount of grief. I think you and all of us have had enough of that. Take what you need and let go of the rest. We cannot change the past, we can only take lessons from our actions, and continue to live the best life possible. What doesn't kill you makes you stronger. Although a metaphor, if that were really true, you would be Hercules!

I wanted to also share with you how family counseling at Sundown M Ranch really changed me. I left a different, and I think, a better person than when I arrived. It was a very healing experience for me. I had a lot of anxiety about what was going to happen, what was going to be said, how much blame will I get, etc. The finest hour, in my opinion, was the one on one meeting we had with you when you finally, finally, finally, opened up to us, and actually talked to us instead of the wall of silence and tears. I was emotionally drained, and we still had some tears, in fact quite a lot of tears, but they were the cleansing ones rather than the crippling tears that I have shed for so many years, in result of your actions.

So, what was it like for me? At times it was a hellish nightmare, and others like Heaven on Earth. You are a bright star. I'm still convinced that you are destined for great things. Don't be in too big of a hurry to get there and light up the sky. You have a lot of healing left within your heart. These hurts did not develop overnight, nor will they be resolved overnight.

Thank you for including me in this effort. I sincerely appreciate your love and recognition of my role, as someone who loves and cares about you, and has always been there for you. I look forward to the continual re-building of our relationship and the eventual complete healing of your body and spirit. Plus I'm anxious to play grandma to your future children, God willing.

Love, Linda

Dear Mark,

What I've noticed is how very different you see the past from what I see and remember. What I understand that you are trying to do is show the world how you saw life through a filter of abandonment and rejection. My understanding is that you are trying to convey that, although this is what you remember now, that was not necessarily the reality of the situation as a whole.

You mention that we never raised our voices. WOW! I remember exactly the opposite. We were ALL always yelling. I remember you yelling so bad at me!!! One time you hauled off and hit me so hard you cracked my sternum!!! Do you remember that? We were all always fighting and arguing, but not in a bad, I hate you way. We just disagreed a lot. We'd fight and scream and yell, and then five minutes later we were all best friends, trying to decide what we would do now!

As I read your story, you need to remember that you were not the only victim in this family. Do you know that before we left Washington, I was contemplating suicide? The strain of the divorce and the intense fear I felt because of the sexual abuse I had suffered, were really taking their toll on my life.

Moving to Hawaii was the best thing Mom could have done for me. I may be dead today if she hadn't done that. Some of what you found to be difficult actually saved my life! I know this is your story, but it is also OUR story, all of us, so it might be good to keep that in mind as you share some of these things. I'm not criticizing you. I just want to put things in perspective. AGAIN, it doesn't mean you shouldn't write from your perspective, but please make it clear that this is what you are saying, it's YOUR perspective.

You need to also understand that dad rarely called US. You're making mom sound so awful when you talk about the phone calls. In reality, I was the one that called him every month and asked him to pay the child support. Otherwise, he wouldn't send it if I did not do this. It was a horrible situation to be in, and I know that dad was very angry about it, but it was the ONLY way we could get him to pay it. We couldn't afford all the lawyers fees to go to court once again, just to get a months support. I think it was his way of getting back at mom, but not realizing that the ones it really affected was us! It also hurt mom to have me call. I remember begging her to let me call and she'd say "Let's just wait one more day, maybe it will come."

After a while dad finally started sending $200 regularly (this was not what had been allotted by the court, but it was better than nothing). Unfortunately, this began after we had been in Hawaii for a while. Yews, there were sometimes we did call him to ask him to help pay for our summer trips. But this is something a child should be able to do. Also, I remember clearly that whenever I told mom I wanted to call dad, she would always let me. She never forbade it. In fact at one point, I was so full of hatred for dad, mom got really mad at me and DEMANDED that I honor him as my father. I also remember her reminding us of his birthday and making us call him, and then he was hardly home when we would called. I remember us not ever really knowing what to say to him, which may be part of the reason why you don't remember having very many conversations with him.

Let me add here that I have a wonderful relationship with dad now. He has apologized to me, and we have talked through many things from the past. I have great respect for him and what he has overcome, as well as what he has owned up to. At 16 however, I was ready to cut him off for life, NOT because of anything mom said, but simply because of the things he had said and done to me personally.

I don't know if you realize how very much you and the other kids meant to me as a child. I felt such a deep sense of responsibility for all of you. Do you remember how I used to hug and kiss you guys all the time? You guys would always push me away and tell me to leave you alone, but I wanted to make sure that you knew you were loved. Mom and Dad loved us, but they weren't very affectionate, and they were often gone working. I felt it my responsibility to love you.

I remember when I was 16 years old and you left for Europe for the first time. You must have been about 13 years old. You got on the plane and I bawled my eyes out all the way home! I was SO worried about you! I didn't know how you were going to make it without me! I had every nightmare scenario going through my mind of what might happen to you along the way. It was horrible! I felt SO responsible for you, and I loved you so much!

You have always had a very special place in my heart. I remember one time when I hurt you SO deeply. We were just little kids living in the Elinor house. You and I had fought about something, and I was so mad at you. I said, "I wish we'd never got you!" OH MY GOSH! I've never seen such pain on any face as I saw on yours. Your face contorted into such a look of pain, and then you burst into tears from SO deep inside you! I can still see it as if it were yesterday. I remember feeling SO HORRIBLE! I didn't mean it! I ran to you and threw my arms around you, and hugged you, and kissed you, over and over again, and told you, " I didn't mean it MARKY, I didn't mean it! I'm sorry, I never meant it! I love you so much!" Over and over, I repeated those words and held you while you cried. I swore I would NEVER do that again, and that I would protect you for the rest of my life! It was such a stupid thing to say. To this day when I think about it, I feel SO horrible. I know I said it then, but let me say it again, "I'm so sorry!" I truly didn't mean it. If I had known at that moment how it would hurt you, if I could have imagined even the look that would come over your face, I NEVER would have said it. Those are words I have regretted throughout my entire life.

There are so few things that I can remember doing that hurt others. It's so hard to remember what we've done to others, yet so easy to remember what others have done to us, isn't it? I wish I could remember, simply so that I could ask forgiveness. I don't want anyone to hurt because of things I've done in my immaturity, anger or my own pain. Yet I remember so much easier the pain that's have been done to me. Well, that is one thing that I do remember with such clarity, and it affects me deeply. I'm really so sorry. I do love you SO much!

In terms of the things you have done and are ashamed of, let me just say that I had envisioned worse. I didn't find it shocking simply because I know what goes along with that kind of lifestyle. Please don't feel ashamed around me because of your past. It doesn't bother me a bit. The only thing I feel is deep sadness for what you've had to go through to get to where you are now. I'm really proud of you Mark, and I'm not really sure you get that yet, but I will continue to say it, and hope that one day you will grasp how very much I love you, care about you, and how very proud I am of you for choosing life, and choosing to persevere through the pain to make a better life for yourself. Your humility in sharing your life with us is no small thing, and I appreciate your openness with me.

There was a time when I felt like I was supposed to be praying for you a lot. I had asked God to remind me and once when I was praying there was a song playing called Place In This World. Every time I would hear it I would think of you and often I would break down and cry for you. As I was praying for you this one particular time I told God that from now on whenever I heard that song I would pray for you, not only when I heard the song, but for sure when I heard it. I can't tell you how many times I heard this song after that within a very short period of time.

The kids somehow got a hold of the tape and started playing it over and over. Just THAT song. Then I would get in the car and turn it on and that song would start playing. Both on the radio and when I'd turn the tape deck on! Then I would visit a friend and THAT song would be on. It was literally everywhere I turned and I felt like God was saying, "Shanie, this is serious. Mark needs me more than ever right now, His life is hanging in the balance." I was literally praying for you night and day for about a month. I'd wake up at night and all I could think was PRAY FOR MARK! And I would start interceding. Sometimes it was as if I could feel your pain and it was so deep and so overwhelming and I would just cry for you. Sometimes I would cry so hard I couldn't even pray for you! At those times I felt like God was allowing me to feel His pain for you as well as the pain you were feeling. I can't explain it so much, but I can just say that I felt it so strong!

It was strange in one way, because I never really knew much of anything about what was going on in your life and yet somehow I always knew when I had to pray and that you were in some kind of danger.

God is SO good MARK! He is SO good! Even when you didn't know it and even when you couldn't find Him He was loving you so much and I know that His heart was breaking for you because I felt it so strongly! I had NO reason to feel this way. I was thousands of miles away and yet I KNEW without a doubt that you were suffering. Somehow it was almost always confirmed through mom or Sherri because they would have been going through similar experiences at the same time. Mark, even when you felt so hopeless and lost, we were right there with you in our spirits. God was so faithful to tell us. He never let you go!

Mark, in all honesty. I have ALWAYS been so amazed by you. You have such an incredible personality. You light up the room when you walk into it and you make people want to get up and enjoy life. You are a joy to be around and you are inspiring to listen to. You have wisdom and insight into people and situations that go beyond natural understanding and you have a tenderness that makes a person feel that you really care about them. I have NEVER stopped feeling that way about you or seeing those qualities in you.

Even though I didn't see you that often over the past several years, whenever I did that same Mark was always there. Even when I could see and feel that there was real pain and anguish going on inside of you, there was still that hint of the real Mark coming across and I have always had THAT as my picture of who you are.

I am so sad for you that you have had to go so low in order to be able to come to the place that you are now. I hate the thought that you have considered death as an option, but at the same time, as I told you when I was there in Washington, it is no surprise to me because I have known it for years. I have been praying for you all this time and I KNEW that one day the Mark I know and love would be back. I KNEW it Mark! It was never a question of whether you would or not, only a question of WHEN. I felt such a strong assurance from God about that as I prayed.

I can't even begin to tell you how incredibly happy I am for you! It's so wonderful to see that you ARE finding your place in this world now! I know you still have things to work through and that you will have tough times ahead, but Mark, I KNOW you can do it! And I am there with you all the way. I may be far away physically, but you have my prayers, my encouragement and my ear any time you need it...and even when you don't!

You are a wonderful brother. You are a gift to our family and an extremely important part of who we are AS a family. I know that being adopted has been tough for you to deal with, but Mark, believe me when I say we would have had a huge gaping hole in our family if you hadn't been there!

Thank you for being a part of my life and for allowing me back into yours!

Love,

Shanie

Hi Mark,

You know, I was talking to Dennis last night about all this and it dawned on me, my earliest memory of my childhood was of the night Mom and Dad brought you home. I remember being woken up and either Mom or Suzanne saying that your brother is here. Do you want to come meet him? I got out of bed and went into the living room, and we all played. I don't remember anything before that. Of course I was only 3-years old. Can you imagine how significant that night must have been for me?

Your book talks about not being real close to me. That was a shocker; it hit me like a ton of bricks. There wasn't a time that we didn't do anything together. As young kids everyone thought we were twins. We went to school together, played baseball together, had all the same friends. You were my best friend. I never looked at you any less then my brother, the same way Sherri, and Shanie are my sisters, and I loved you the same also. You were and are my brother. I still remember the day you shot me in the head with BB gun and I pretended to die, and how scared you were. I tell the kids that story all the time. Probably because Joshua has a very weak BB gun also.

I truly believe that you make mom out to be the bad guy in this whole situation. If you had really read her letter to you at the very start of this book, I think you would have seen her differently. It made me cry, and hope that someday when I get the opportunity to adopt, I feel the same excitement and love she felt for you. You make her out to be a radical Christian, like we were in some kind of cult. You made her out to be extremely neglectful to us kids. I seriously disagree with you there also.

I can remember her taking us to swimming lessons and being there the whole time. I remember her coming to all of our baseball games. I remember her working with our youth groups, as one of the leaders, and opening up our home for youth functions so she could be with us. I remember her supporting you 100% in gymnastics and scrimping and saving every penny she could so she could be in Honolulu with you for your gymnastics competition. I remember her going to work with the men in our church back in Washington to work out in the cold wet woods doing something with trees so she could have money for our Christmas. I remember her giving each one us kids $20.00 at to go shopping for Christmas presents for each other. I remember her sitting with us on the dining room table doing arts and crafts with us over the holidays, and making all sorts of Christmas goodies. I remember her taking us to the drive in movies, or to the mall for a pizza and a movie. I remember her taking you to purchase your first car. I remember how scared she was the night she got the call about you and Sherri being in that car accident. She woke me up shaking and pacing the floor waiting for you two to come home. I remember her making those costumes for us in the parade and the hours spent doing each one. She even had to redo mine. Remember, I was going to be Grover and it didn't turn out, so I had to be Harry. I recall us choosing who we wanted to be. How about the Wizard of Oz? You had a very creative costume as Tin Man (I had to be the witch, I wanted to be Dorthy and have the shining shoes). And people didn't throw us candy, we threw people candy. I also remember her working late nights to put food on the table for us so we wouldn't have to be on welfare.

Mark mom was a very supportive mother. I don't know where you got the idea she wasn't there for us. And her having to work when we were really little that wasn't her choice. By the time we were in first grade she wasn't working any more and was always home with us. She had her moments, and she wasn't perfect. Take it from a mother of five without a husband/dad in the home. It isn't an easy job. We're bound to screw up every once in a while. I can't imagine having to do it alone. I can't imagine what it must be like to find out the man you are supposed to spend your life with is having affairs and does not want to give them up to save his marriage. What would you expect mom to have done? Put on a happy face and act like everything is peachy keen? Well it doesn't work like that.

This is something to think about because you made the one and only parent in your life that has never abandoned you out to be the one who has. Not once in your book did you mention dad and his affairs. You could bring up the crap about mom's second husband but you couldn't talk about your father never being there for our birthdays, or that he wouldn't send the child support checks, and when he did they weren't what he was ordered to pay? You forgot to mention that his other family was living high on life and got all the fancy clothes, and games, and toys and trips, boats, the house, etc., while mom had to give our home back to the bank? For mom to buy us a candy bar was a treat because she couldn't afford to do that. Or how about the fact that it was going around Shelton that poor Brad and Linda couldn't have a life because his ex-wife and kids are sucking everything they have. Hmmm, I don't remember us having squat. You also failed to mention how awful the Willis's treated you, and the rest of us for that matter. And how he (g-pa Willis) threatened mom with us kids. How about how they never even knew we existed after we moved to Hawaii? Or what about the Christmas we spent with dad's family, and they piled Royce with gifts. All they gave us was a sweat suit. And a very ugly one at that. Royce wasn't even dad's kid. Mark I could go on and on about how unfair you are being to mom, but there are other situations that I need to write about.

I need to let you know that the things I said about dad were not said in a way to hurt him, or that I don't love him, or to make him out to be the devil. It is said because it needs to be noted. You cannot put all that in there about mom and not say very much about him, he caused a lot of this. I know he has a lot of regrets. Who doesn't? I personally think you are keeping it out because of whom he is, and because you have always wanted to be accepted by him. You have always wanted to please him, and in a way, I think you wanted to be like him. I love dad, and I hold no ill will towards him today.

Anyway, when we lived in Purdy you had moved in with us, all though we were advised not to do it, I couldn't turn my back on my brother so we did. You were embarrassed by the little we had so you had gone out and purchased at least a few hundred dollars worth of stuff for the house. Not realizing that it had been with stolen money or I wouldn't have accepted it. Then there was the case of the spending our rent money. We hadn't had a checking account at the time so you would deposit Dennis's checks for us in your account and then write us out a check for rent. Then one day Dennis has our landlord show up at his work wanting his rent with a fee added to it. He doesn't know what's going on so he calls home and I had to tell him you spent the rent money. I can't remember how it all transpired but you came to me one day and told me you don't have the rent. You had spent it, but you were working something out with dad. He gave you the money in advance to cover the rent and you would work it off in his store. Well you spent that money also and I was keeping it from Dennis because I was afraid of what he might do to you. But now it had all come crashing down on my head and it wasn't pretty.

Then there was the phone bill every phone call was long distance and you were calling your friends left and right and we couldn't afford it, the bill had gotten up to $300.00 plus. It was shut off, but by then we were moving to Bellingham so you moved in with a friend. That didn't last long and you were up in Bellingham with us. That's when I got pregnant with Joshua (that info was wrong) during that time Dennis was working for the car wash and had gotten you hired there also. He eventually got a job a TrendWest Resort and you stayed on at the car wash. (While we were in Purdy, Grandpa Schmidt had taken us shopping for a car and co-signed for us with the Buick. We hadn't acquired credit in the state so we couldn't get a loan approved). You had wanted to go back to Shelton/Olympia to see friends for the weekend so we let you use the car. You had borrowed it a few times for those weekend trips and finally one day it didn't make it home. We never did find out the true reason for it breaking down, but we had are suspicions, anyway there was some kind of hole underneath it. Well grandpa took the car cause we couldn't afford to fix it, but we took crap from just about every family member over the whole car situation. Actually I should say Dennis was treated very unfair with the whole thing. He was the one blamed for it all. Till this day we don't know why the car busted down. We had maintained it. Anyway we left in Sept to go back to Hawaii. That's pretty much where my life ends with you.

One last thing with mom and Ywam. We were very privileged to have been involved with Kings Kids. You got to travel all around the world, go to communist countries, see Olympic stadiums, meet and make friends with people across the world. How many kids do you know get an opportunity to do something like that? We were blessed. It wasn't a ploy to keep us away from dad, we still spent part of the summers with him. And the only time any of us called dad for money besides Shanie doing it for the late child support checks, was when we were doing an outreach and we needed funding to help get us there. If other people could give us money to help, why shouldn't our own father, it's his parental responsibility. We weren't begging for money either. The way we raised money for those trips is the same way my kids raise money to help their teams go to Nationals for cheer or other youth type events. There is no shame in doing that.

I really believe you need to do some soul searching and ask God to show you the truth about your childhood, because you really have your facts and memories mixed up. And I think this is affecting Adam in a negative way and he is using your situations to find things in Him that aren't really issues. I don't know if I made that clear, but for example, he states in his letter to you that he was forced to go to the orphanage in Korea when he really didn't want to and that he had to put on a fake smile like he was happy about it. That is not true. You two were given the option and you chose not to and Adam was to thrilled about going. I was in Korea also. He came back from that orphanage ecstatic because they had pictures of him he had never seen before. His whole attitude changed after that. Don't you remember how he locked himself in the bathroom and refused to come out? He went almost crazy when we first got to Korea and no one could really comfort him. Mom had gotten sent back to Japan with part of the group while we were sent on to Korea. Me, You, Sherri, and Adam mom were so upset because they had separated us from her. So it was when she finally got to Korea she asked or you had asked if it would be possible to see the orphanage. You backed out, but Adam wanted to go. I think he is trying to find reasons to be angry with mom, especially now that he has such a wonderful relationship with dad. Both of you have hurt her with this and again <u>I want to remind you that she wasn't the one who abandon you ever!</u> I'm not saying this to make mom out to be miss perfect mother, I say it to hopefully open your eyes to some reality....

Honestly you sound very angry in the book, and I understand that you probably were during the time you were writing it. It did after all start out as a journal. I just think you have a lot to still work out and you have a lot more inner healing that needs to take place before this book can be finished and used to help someone in the same situation as you. You titled it Suffering in Silence, and if I were someone who was suffering, I would pick this book up and read it in hopes that you could help me. To know that someone else has suffered the way I have, and to know he made it through, and is doing good today. That's what I would hope to find in your book. Encouragement knowing I'm not alone and there is hope. But I'm not getting that. I believe it can be like that, but there's just so much more for you to do before it can be completed.

I want you to understand that writing this was not in any way to hurt you. But when I read your book a lot of the things you talked about didn't fit. I understand it is from your standpoint, but even then I think you had a lot of it misqude. You need to know I am not angry with you, never have been. I do love you always have and always will. You are my brother and that will never change. The happy memories of you and me growing up will always be in my heart and cherished. I don't say these things to hurt or anger you I say them because I care and because I want this book to be successful, and because I want you to truly discover the real you, and to find that perfect peace.

I found a picture of you yesterday by my phone. I guess it had been in my address book and fell out. It was of you in Korea wearing the Chinese outfit Caz's grandparents lent you. We had to take individual pictures of us in our costumes. I have to tell you, you look pretty happy in this picture you are actually laughing. That was a wonderful summer however the first night in Hong Kong freaked me out, and I wasn't particularly fond of the Philippines, but I would never trade that summer for anything. How about that big mall in Korea we got to go to, or those Popsicles we bought from the street vendors and we thought they were Strawberry, but in fact they were red bean. yuck!. They did actually have Strawberry and watermelon, etc we just had to learn to pick the right one. In Hong Kong we would go to McD's and a Big Mac would cost $8.00. In fact it was like .20 US. Hong Kong money is called Dollar also. It would seem so expensive and yet it was so cheap.

So, back to growing up, I don't think we were the "Brady Bunch" family, I just don't think we were as dysfunctional as it sounds in your book. You mention that people like us/me owe society more. Well I work with youth everyday. Not just in the church. I work with them because I have a heart for them and because I don't want them to choose the same path you did. I work with kids who have divorced parents, who have parents in prison, who have parents that have committed suicide, have parents that have died from cancer, parents are alcoholics, or drug addicted parents etc. I work with kids from all walks of life. I give them hope. I show them that there is something greater for them out there, and there is a purpose for their life. I am giving back to society.

You asked me to share how I found solace, My solace was in God I never turned my back on Him. He say's He will never leave me, nor forsake me. So why then should I abandon Him? I chose to keep Him in my life.

If there is one thing I've learned from mom it's to be a straight shooter. To stand up for what I believe in. It may have taken time to develop but as I get older and raise my own children I have found it getting easier to open my mouth and say what needs to be said. And that's why I have said what I have in this letter to you. I don't want to sugar coat my feelings.

I want to end with this scripture out of Ephesians. I pray it speaks to you. It's Ephesians1:4-14: "For He chose us in Him before the creation of the world to be holy, and blameless in His sight. In love he predestined us to be adopted as his sons through Jesus Christ, in accordance with His pleasure, and will - to the praise of His glorious grace, which He has freely given us in the One He loves. In Him we have redemption through His blood, the forgiveness of sins, in accordance with the riches of God's grace that He lavished on us with all wisdom and understanding. And He made known to us the mystery of His will according to His good pleasure, which He purposed in Christ, to be put in effect when the times will have reached their fulfillment - to bring all things in heaven and on earth together under one head, even Christ. In Him we were also chosen, having been predestined according to the plan of him who works out everything in conformity with the purpose of His will, In order that we who were the first to hope in Christ, might be for the praise of His glory. And you also were included in Christ when you heard the word of truth, the gospel of your salvation. having believed we were marked in Him with a seal, the promised Holy Spirit, who is a deposit guaranteeing our inheritance until the redemption of those who are God's possession - to the praise of his Glory."

Love, Dana

Dear Mark,

You asked me to write about our life together—good and bad—and how your life impacted me. s far back as I can remember, I always thought of you as my brother. There's a bond I have with you that is no different from my bond with Shanie, Dana, and Adam. I have always felt that bond with you. No matter what you ever did or will do can ever change the love I feel towards you as my brother; I love you simply because you are my brother.

First, I don't remember the day that you came into our family because I was only two years old (you were three years old). But I do remember playing with you at a young age. We used to play "house". You would agree to play "house" with me ONLY if your "kids" were your stuffed animals. You did NOT want the dolls. I would agree to that since I really wanted someone to play "house" with. We used to play in your red, white, and blue bedroom, which was across the hall from my mint green bedroom at the "white house" in Washington.

In the summer, we would play baseball with our neighborhood friends in our big grassy yard (you seemed to always hit the ball so far), try to build forts out of the wood from the fallen down shed in the vacant field, and hike and explore through the woods until we reached the apple orchard (You were more adventurous than I was, so you would lead and I would follow).

In the winter, we would do activities like cut out pilgrim costumes out of brown paper bags and make instruments out of cardboard boxes and rubber bands.

I thought of you as happy, smart, curious, funny, creative, and liked by others. I saw a lot of your qualities when you and your friend, Andy, pretended to be disk jockeys and recorded yourselves DJing between the hit songs of the time. You even made your own tape covers. I still have one of those tapes you made. I kept it because I thought it would be fun some day for you to show your future wife and children a glimpse of you as a child. Can you believe it's been almost 20 years since you made those tapes?

Those were some of the good times I remember. I also have memories of experiences that were difficult to deal with at the time. You and I were still elementary school age when mom and dad separated and later divorced. Although I didn't know it at the time, we felt similarly about the divorce but kept our feelings inside. I remember all of us kids being told by mom and our pastors that mom and dad were divorcing. We all cried together. Then all of us kids went upstairs while the adults stayed downstairs to talk. You, Shanie, Dana and, I think, Adam, were playing in the hall laughing as if nothing had happened. I was not happy about that! I wanted to be sad and grieve. I couldn't believe how you could be so happy in such a sad time. You were in the hall climbing up the hall wall (literally). Do you remember how we use to do that? You would put one foot on each wall as if doing the splits and climb up to the ceiling. Later our pastor came upstairs and saw you and Dana climbing the wall and laughing. He said that he was so glad to see us playing. I thought, "how can you say that when my parents are not together anymore!" From that moment on, I learned to hide how I really felt about the divorce. I learned later that I wasn't alone. You were hiding your true feelings as well. I wish now that you and I would've talked about our feelings of sadness and loss. Years later, I had to grieve mom and dad's divorce so that I could move on with that part of my life.

Soon after the divorce was finalized, Dad married Linda. Their marriage was difficult for me to accept at first. I felt so uncomfortable at their wedding. I didn't know Linda, and I felt jealous of Royce. I thought, "How can he [Dad] replace us so quickly?" Here was another situation that you and I shared similar feelings but just didn't talk about it. Although I didn't realize it at the time, these two events changed the way I reacted, thought, and felt about both people and life in general; they shaped who I am today.

I also have some not so good memories growing up together. They are not memories that scarred me or anything, just memories that stuck with me as I got older. I guess I see them as normal childhood behaviors that have the opportunity to teach us lessons when we are younger. They are circumstances that can influence how we make choices later on.

There were times that I saw that you could be sneaky and a little devious. I remember when we still lived at the "white house" (we were early elementary age) and you took mom and dad's valuable coins to purchase some candy bars that we were selling for school. I decided to use the coins as well. You got caught. I didn't. I never admitted to it because I didn't want to get in trouble but felt so guilty about it. I never wanted to feel that shame again.

There was another time I realized that you would try to make me feel important to use me to get what you wanted. When we were living in the subsidized housing in Hawaii (we were around early teen age) we were both in our own rooms in bed. You said you had something important to ask me, as if you wanted my advice. So I got out of bed and stood at your doorway as you asked me a few questions. After I answered them, I started to turn away to go to bed. You stopped me and said, "Oh, can you turn off my light?" I realized at that moment that you called me over to shut your light off. You didn't want to get out of bed. I was so annoyed with you. The next night you tried it again, but I didn't fall for it. You were surprised that I had caught on.

When we were mid-teens and being home schooled, mom would tell us to go take our school tests. You would go into the storage closet under the stairs and sneak the answer key to your test. I couldn't understand why you didn't want to learn. It made me so mad that you were cheating. I wanted so badly to learn and be taught because I didn't want to be stupid by the time I got out on my own. I thought you would've felt the same way.

Well regardless of how we came up with our answers to our tests, we both had to take basic classes all over again once we started college. Also, we both had to take what felt like a million math classes in order to get to a college level math class. And we both put off our math classes until the last year of college. It's ironic that we both had jobs that worked with numbers; you were an auditor, and I was a financial services specialist. Thank goodness for calculators and computers!

For the most part though, I remember you as being good. I really don't remember any fights we had, although, I'm sure we did fight as all brothers and sisters do. But, what I have come to see more and more as I reflect back is that you hid a lot of your behaviors and feelings giving the illusion that you were *the happy go lucky kid.*

Together we had a both life defining and bonding moment when we were teens—I was 15 and you were 16 years old. It was when we went to the youth retreat. While we were at the retreat, I had a moment where I realized how valuable life was and that it was truly a gift from God. I recognized that I needed to be thankful for the life given to me—I felt an urgency to pray. I needed to ask God's forgiveness because two weeks prior I had asked God to take my life; I had asked God to take me to be with him if there was nothing on earth to live for. I later found out that around the same time, you had prayed asking God to take your life as well. That night on our way home from the retreat, we got into a car accident that should have killed or left us both critically injured. I remember the details of the accident, but I won't go into them right now.

What I will go into is what happened after the accident. We were on that dark, quiet rode, miles from home. We started walking home. I was in shock and kept shaking so you put your arm around me as we walked. When your arm was around me my shaking would stop; I couldn't walk unless your arm was around me. It meant a lot to me that you wanted to help and comfort me. You and I were never real affectionate with each other, but in a time of need, you were there for me, and I was grateful for that.

However, the most important thing to remember is that we both prayed right before the accident asking God to take our lives, but instead he chose not to. He has a purpose for us here on earth. We need to remember to use our life the way God wants us to because he has put us here for a reason. We may never fully grasp what the exact purpose is, but all we can do is rely on God for wisdom, direction, and strength.

A few years after the accident, you and I were living in Washington. I was in Bellingham going to college and I think you were in Shelton working. Although I did not know it at the time, you were making a lot of bad choices, drinking, stealing, and hanging out with the wrong crowd. I remember waking up in the middle of the night with a strong sense to pray for you. I couldn't sleep. I was really concerned about you and felt you were not safe. So, I prayed for your safety. This happened more than once. I really believe God has been watching out for you. He has <u>never</u> let you go nor forgotten you. Even though everything in this world is inconsistent and with fault, God will always stay the same. He will always be there when no one else is. I found security during the hard times in my life knowing that He would be faithful when I needed to rest in His arms.

I remember when I was living at "The Mansion" while in college; I received a phone call from you. You were in jail. You wanted money, but I wouldn't give it. You had borrowed money before and had never paid it back. I was not about to give you more money. But I would be there to encourage and support you. I decided I would visit you while you were in the Whatcom County jail. I was the only family you had in Whatcom County, so I made sure I did not miss your visitations. I hoped that jail time would be your wake-up call.

I had never been in a jail before. I went by myself to visit you. Each time it felt eerie as I walked in, gave my identification, waited for the door to unlock, walked down the quiet corridor that echoed with every sound made, sat in the small cubicle with a window separating us, and picked up the phone to the left of me that I would use to talk to you. If you weren't there in the booth already, I would wait for you to come to your side of the window. We talked. You cried. You cried every time I came. You hated the choices you had made. You were in so much pain. I wanted so badly to help you. I thought you were serious about getting your life together (and maybe you were at the time), but soon after you got released from jail, you started your self-destructive cycle all over again. You became more and more disconnected, hardened, and unwilling. All I could be was available and prayerful.

Another time I thought you might be at a turning point was when I visited you in the boot camp detention center. You seemed to be getting counseling that worked, put in a position to build your self-worth, and ultimately given the tools and strength to overcome your struggles. This too did not last.

My final effort to help you was when Dad, Linda, Adam, Matt, and I all agreed to have a family intervention with you. You had used all of us at one time or another and you were in trouble once again with drinking, drugs, money…. We confronted you and you seemed defensive. You finally gave in (what seemed against your will) in order to get help and get your life back on the right road. Matt and I opened our house up to you as long as you were getting your life back together. But things didn't change. You would come home in the middle of the night either drunk or high (that's what we were pretty sure of, but hoped was not true).

One day while we were sitting at my dining room table, I asked you how you were REALLY doing. You got so mad and defensive. You didn't want to change. In fact you were going to some sort of mandatory alcohol or chemical dependency support group, but you thought it was a joke. You would tell us that you didn't think you had a drinking problem. You were in such denial.

Mark, I feel I know you more than you realize. As time went on, I learned your behaviors and patterns. I knew when you were making wrong choices, addicted and using, making excuses, blaming, lost and running away. You didn't want to hear what I had to say and didn't want help; you only wanted to use everyone for your advantage. Do you remember when you asked me for gas money so that you could get to work? I thought, "How ridiculous that he needs money for gas when he makes twice the money as me and he only supports himself." Matt and I agreed that you probably had spent your money on alcohol, drugs or gambling, or you spent it on gas and wanted our money for alcohol, drugs or gambling. After you had gotten so defensive at me at the dining room table, I was afraid to confront you. I was so stressed at work, in my second trimester of pregnancy, and couldn't handle the deception we were living in at home, so Matt agreed to ask you to leave. He told you it was because we needed the space for the baby. As I have already told you, I do regret not being upfront and honest with you. I was afraid we would wrongly accuse you and so didn't confront you. In retrospect, we were not wrong at all.

I don't bring this memory up to cause you pain and regret. You have already asked forgiveness, and we have forgiven you. I only bring it up as part of my story of our life together and of how your life affected me.

Mark, you and I have had several heart to heart talks over the last 12-years. You have opened up many times about your abandonment, life struggles, and hurts from the divorce. I love those talks because you were honest, real, vulnerable, and so close to facing what you were running from. I longed for you to deal with those pains. I hated to see you so wounded. I wanted to help but didn't know how. I guess you just weren't ready or you just didn't know how to help yourself.

You declined more and more the last 3-years of your self-destructive behaviors. You had roommate after roommate, dodged bill collectors, missed birthdays and holidays with family, and displayed odd behavior (acting tired one minute and then hyper the next or vise versa). You would hide behind your job and talk about your promotions and accomplishments. I saw right through it. To be honest, I felt you needed to loose your job in order to have your lifestyle exposed and changed because it was too convenient for you to hide behind it. In fact, I even told Matt this. It's interesting that it took loosing your job to get you to where you are now.

When I was told that you were going to Sundown M Ranch, I was glad you were getting help, but to be honest, not too optimistic about the future. However, you have really proven that you are serious this time. You seem to really understand yourself more now. You're admitting your weaknesses, facing your demons, and seeking forgiveness and reconciliation with family and God. You know you have wounds that need both addressing and healing. You may be afraid to face them but not unwilling. Your emotions are raw and honest. I love that about you. I'm proud of you for making choices that will help you to stay clean; like staying in Yakima, keeping your support network, and dealing with your hurts from the abandonment and divorce. You've chosen to write a book even in the midst of criticism in order to help yourself and others to heal. You're finding purpose.

I want you to know that I am here for you. I love getting your emails and phone calls and hearing about how you are doing. I want to be a support to you. You can share your true feelings. Nothing you can say can take my love or commitment away from you. Remember to keep your focus, keep your life well balanced. Learn what true success is and what the purpose of life is. I love you and am so thankful that you, my brother, have had the strength to rely on God and come to a place of healing and reconciliation!

Your sister,

Sherri

Hi Mark,

It's amazing how little I really know about you. I think that it's a real blessing in disguise that you went from being a zero to being something important. Don't worry about what others think about you, or your past, or where you're going too. Once you finish you can finally say that you've done it. So much for making that great thriller. Congratulations-you have just lived it and are living proof. I'm really proud of you and so is Miranda. We know that life is not always fair, but I wouldn't have wanted it any different.

But regarding some of the things you have written about. It's been a long time waiting and Miranda has been helping me along to finally say some things to you. You are right in a lot of things and wrong in so many more. I think the only way that I have not done or been in the same situations as you are by your example. Growing up, I really didn't remember you being around after I turned thirteen. This was right after we had come back from the 1988 Olympics in Korea. This is ironic, because this is where a lot of my fears came to light. I don't know if you remember this, but mom had taken me to the orphanage in Pusan, Korea, where I was supposedly living before I was brought to the states for the first time.

I felt a tremendous sense of fear and anger. I didn't know what to do and how to act. If you look at a lot of pictures of me during our trip there. I was never really smiling. I was irritable with mom because I didn't know what to feel and to think. I just remember that I had to act a certain way since we were on King's Kids and it would reflect badly on the team if I wasn't be enjoyable. Mom didn't know that I was really building a sort of resentment that would later be more apparent in mine and your life. We actually just talked about it recently.

Growing up in a white society, I didn't look the part, but acted the part. I think we both have cast doubt and disbelief to so many people. I have to think and believe that when most people talk to you or me, they half expect us to be like most Asians they encounter. Once we show our intelligent side, we are like royalty to them and then they can respect us. In my sociology class at South Puget Sound, we discussed race, and one individual mentioned terms we use to identify the races.

They called me a banana, I said, "What!". He said that I was yellow on the outside and white on the inside. I didn't agree verbally with them and but had to agree inside. This was who I was. I had detached myself from the person that I truly am. I am still Korean no matter what I do. But socially, I am this person that overcame my barrier of looking inferior in my own eyes. To this day I still have a hard time socializing with any type of Asians and have no true friends that are except for you. But even as having you as a brother as we had talked a few months back, deep down inside we both felt the same way weird way about each other. You were still another Asian to me.

It's amazing that we have come to this and I wished so many people could understand that its not even in just our own race but in many different forms. Whether you are not adopted into the same family, look different, age gaps, gender bias, and same race lighter skin. We live in a racist and non-binding society. I had a short conversation with an African American woman I worked with a very long time ago.

Story:
A customer comes in looking for a particular sales person, but not sure what she looks like other than African American. The sales associate answering the inquiry answers that the customer is looking for the Darker skinned African American woman sales associate. And she said it like this. I asked her on a break later on why she referred to her as the Darker African American woman instead of by her name of Yvonne. She fell silent and said that she didn't know and walked off. I

saw a perfect example of what a socially imperfect people we are. I tend to call it In House Racism.

Going back to what I was talking about before. You led a life that I never really knew, other than what mom told me and how you needed help. Mom once told me how you were in jail and how you would need money and if I would be willing to help you out. I had some money, I think about $300 that she thought would help out a lot since dad had refused to help you out. So I gave her the money and that was that. I never expected it back, but I guess we both are even over the ages, since we have been going back and forth on the money thing for a while. Its kind of like the I've got this one covered and you get the next round.

But ultimately, I never truly understood why you kept on getting in trouble. The more I heard, the more I wanted to find out why you did the things you did. Once I saw this part of you that we have talked about, I never really could say no to you on a lot of things. I looked up to you even though it felt weird to be helping you. Everyone always said to not help you, because it wasn't helping you. I supposed I was being cautious in some regards, but later in life we met upon some incidents where we both went through hard times.

Your whole entire life has been spent with me being the spectator and choosing whether or not I was going to follow down the same path. But your failures became my reason for not going down the same paths as yours. I do have my own faults that I am not proud of. But if you hadn't done what you have done, things would not be what they are now. You would not be where you are now. And there are many other choices that we all have made that might have changed our own outcomes. Your actions were very vital to us sacrificing what little bit of emotions that we to obtain from you. I never really knew what kind of roller coaster ride you were going to take me on.

I know you probably regret this, but I used to have a very hard time whenever you called because I always feared that you were calling about money and something that you needed help with. It's like that movie with Robert Downey Junior-Less Than Zero. Sometimes going from 100 to zero and slowly back up again is the only real way that you can find your peace of mind. You had everything and made the right choice giving up your lifelong dreams. You still have this to fall upon, which many people do not. Take things one at a time. And from this you shall conquer all. You still have many personal issues such as I do, that deals with our adoptions. This may take awhile.

Love lots, your bro.

Adam

Dear Mark,

I don't remember much about my biological father Larry. My mom never pushed her feelings of him to me. My mom would encourage me to try and have a relationship with him. Otherwise, I don't remember much about my parents divorce. I was a very small child and it was a confusing time. When my mom met my dad, well, your dad, the first memory I have is the wedding. During these hard times of dealing with my feelings, Brad, my dad, was always there for me even though Larry was not.

My next memory was with all of you coming from Hawaii for your summer visits. I always felt like Sherri didn't like me, Dana didn't really care one way or the other; and Shanie was never around so I don't really know her that well. I knew all the kids weren't accepting my mom. You were the only one I remember reaching out. I felt like you cared. We had a lot in common. We both felt like we didn't belong. You were adopted and I was the new brother. We each knew each other were different, even though we never talked much about how we felt, we just both knew.

I am also 95% sure you taught me how to ride a bike. Do you remember? Down the alley of the Ellinor house? The bike was yellow with red flames? You would push me down the alley. I would tell you not to let go. You would laugh and say I was doing it on my own. I would look back and get scared because you weren't there and then would crash. I kept falling and scraping my hands. That is one of my most personable memories. Parents are supposed to do this. But they were really busy. People ask me how close we are. I tell them that story.

I can't quite pinpoint the exact time that you moved in but I have a lot of memories with you in the Cloquallum house. I remember when you had that pizza delivery job. Maybe for a week? I also remember your uniform from the yogurt store you had worked at in Hawaii was always laying around. We had a little thing. Remember, you would come home from work from dad's store and we would set traps for each other. Booby traps. Then I would run into the bathroom and you would lock me in. I would try and open the door but you had tied it to the bedroom door handle. That was our bonding as brothers. I remember being very envious of you doing gymnastics. I was very jealous that you could do a back flip and all the girls would want to hang out with you. It didn't matter where we were. That was the coolest. For some reason when I think back, I don't have a lot of memories with the other kids. Most of my memories are with you. As you got older and started meeting new friends, I tried to hang out with you. In the beginning you always let me come along. It was a warm feeling because I didn't feel like I belonged. Even though you were growing older, you still tried to include me. Then, as we got older Linda, my mom, and dad's marriage became acceptable. All the kids began to tolerate me.

The first time I can remember wanting to grow up real fast. You had a party in the barn. You guys played music, had a dance and a whole bunch of friends over. It was that moment I wanted to be like you. I followed in your footsteps a lot. You were starting to change though. You would spend more time with your friends. I got left behind a lot. I remember I wanted to grow up so bad so I could still hang out with you. I didn't want to lose the bond we had growing up. It was the same year you started driving a lot. You had the jeep. You started partying more. That's when you stared getting in to real trouble. Dad was upset. You kept beating up his jeep. Taking it into the woods, or stump jumping, as they referred to it. I wanted you to take me places with you. It was very confusing that we were all so separate. Especially since I was getting so close to you. The other kids weren't around, and then you left. I couldn't understand why you would go out with your friends all the time and I couldn't go. I would wait at home for you. I would set my traps. Our traps. Then you would stay out later, and later. Then you wouldn't come home. That's when I started to get into art. I drew all the time. I made a character that is still in my drawings today. It was kind of my new friend. Then I remember you had that Isuzu impulse, kind of a sports car. I remember when you drove it into the ditch. Dad was so mad.

Then I remember dad asked me if I wanted to be adopted? Then my inferiorities of not belonging didn't matter for a while. I was an Owen. Finally I belonged. Then I had the chicken pox the night of the adoption party.

Then the next memory of us was living together in the blue house in the downstairs. I remember how mad dad was when you got your first credit card. I think you bought that huge home stereo. I wanted one too because you had one. I looked up to you. I followed whatever you did. Remember I bought the cheap one? I saved up all my allowance money. I liked it so much, I was so proud. Remember I set it up right next to the headboard of my bed? I remember we would have stereo wars. It was like we were brothers again. I remember we would lay on the ground with all the lights out listening to Queensryche. I don't remember the exact song but if I heard it today I would remember it. We would lay for hours listening to music and watching the laser you had connected to your stereo that would throw images all over the ceiling and walls to the beats of the music. I remember during this time your friends were fading out of your life and you were staying home a lot more. You started school again and did a lot of homework at your desk with the desk lamp on. I played music really quiet trying not to bug you. But I did. This is also the time we went through the art phase. This was a really fun time for me. We would draw all over the downstairs wall in ink that could only be seen in the black light. You thought it was so cool the idea you had of the man that you drew that was running into the wall. I remember that you were a great writer too. You used to write poems. You wouldn't let anybody read very many of them. I remember one poem you wrote on the wall. I remember reading it and how much in awe I was at how you could write. Then yourstarted writing your first story on dad's really old computer. I remember you being so excited. You were going to write a book. Then I remember your friends coming back into your life. You hung out with me less and less. You stopped writing. We stopped being brothers again. These are some of the last really happy child hood memories I have with you.

I remember crying for the very first time as brothers. You told me to leave you alone. It was a Saturday night. You had some girls over. You took my black light into the sauna and kicked me out. I remember crying that night. Still to this day, you have not told me why you kicked me out of the sauna. We were always best pals until your friends would come over. Our relationship made me feel like I belonged. Dad was always busy. Always gone. Meeting after meeting. You looked after me. Why did you kick me out of the sauna?

I remember the second time I cried. I don't know how it started. But I think I got into your stuff. You went upstairs for dinner. I felt betrayed. I laid your speakers on the floor. Remember? No one was allowed to touch your stereo. I wanted it to look like I threw them on the ground. But I didn't. I remember 15-minutes later, I went upstairs and you went back downstairs. Then you yelled and made me come back downstairs. You pushed me and yelled at me. You didn't hit me though. I remember feeling like I did something really wrong. I was sad. I didn't want you to be mad at me. I still cannot even remember why we even started arguing in the first place. Then we grew up.

I remember a really big party. I think our parents were in Europe. At that party there was a lot of drinking. I remember I had a friend over that night. I don't remember who it was. I remember a lot of people there. I remember alcohol all over. I thought of the trouble you could get in but never said anything. I stayed out of it. I also helped you clean up. I don't remember what my friend and I did during the party. I remember you didn't want me around during the party. I think you made us stay downstairs. In those days it seemed like you knew you were headed for trouble, but looked out for me. Then for some reason mark, after that time in life things really messed me up. I remember you moving to Bellingham. I remember being sad. You were leaving. The dates in my head are really confused. I still to this day don't remember being mad at you going to jail. I remember being in the car to pick you up from jail once. I remember your hair was really short. I remember not being mad. Maybe I didn't know the whole story, or maybe the fact that we hadn't talked in a long time. I felt happy to see you.

I remember your car wreck. I was asleep and woken up by my mom. I was really disoriented. She told me to get dressed as fast as I can. Then we all got in the car. I remember them saying, "Marks been in an accident." I don't even remember the drive to the hospital. I just remember feeling like I might lose my brother. All my memories and feelings were going back and forth in my head, I had a bad headache. The ride to the hospital seemed like five hours. It was only on the top of the hill through town maybe 15-miuntes away. We actually got to the waiting area at the hospital and you hadn't even arrived yet. All we knew is that you had been pinned under a car and you were on your way. For the longest time I thought you had just fallen asleep. I didn't know until later the real reason. I was very angry when I found out you were driving drink. I never put two and two together when I saw the sheriff there. I thought he was there because it was an accident. I had to pry it out of my parents to find out alcohol was involved. For the first time in my life I became very angry and sad at that time. I was more angry at the way you made me feel on the way to the hospital. Then you were gone again. You kept coming back, and then leaving again. In and out of my life. I don't remember much except that when ever you were around things usually weren't that good in your life.

For some reason after that I remember my parents building the house. Then you were round again. You, Adam and myself lived in their old house. I really had a fun summer then. We would listen to 80's music. We would open the French doors and you would teach me to do front handsprings in the front yard. Then I remember you and I having a problem with Adam. For a while living there I was working at the theater. Then Adam and I moved into another house. We were all grown up. We all went our separate ways. I think you went to Tacoma with some friends of yours. I didn't see you for a long time after that. Those were the days I would think back to growing up together. Remember back as kids spending the summer at mason lake marina? Remember working at Brad's Quick Stop? We had a blast breaking down boxes in the cooler after stocking the shelves. That's actually where I got my allowance to buy that stereo.

I just remember really looking up to as a kid. Something in common we had is that we were both adopted. It was awesome. I guess now as adults we have a ball every time we get together, we make everyone laugh. I was always told by people when they saw me, where's Mark? That's all I heard. They would say you and Mark together make me laugh. I didn't think we were that funny until Carrie and I started dating and Dave, her dad, came over for a family function.

I remember we were playing pool and making everyone laugh. That was the first time I saw him laugh. It was because we were joking around. We would do one-liners, feeding off each other. You know, I think people would even wet their pants.

Then when you started doing drugs, I became curious. Scarred. Confused. But curious. You became so distant. You didn't seem like the same person anymore. You weren't really setting goals anymore. Growing up you always had ideas, goals, and things in life you were going to accomplish. Remember Washington Bottled Rain? You had countless ideas of stupid nick-knacks to make a million dollars. You knew it could be done. The older you got the less you acted on these ideas. The less it seemed like you cared. When the drugs got involved we stopped hearing about those ides all together. All you started talking about later was money. Your shoes. Your suits. All you talked about was money. You never talked about the exciting ideas you had anymore. It was just money.

As I got older I wasn't really angry at you for not coming too my wedding. I really wanted you there. You said you would be there. You let me down. You were going to be my best mad. That was the one huge thing I wanted you there for. But for some reason I remember not being that mad at you. I think inside I already knew you wouldn't show-up. Maybe I didn't want to get my hopes up. Maybe that's why I wasn't too mad at you. Actually, you didn't go to my adoption party either. Carrie and I talked about this. Were going to pick you up when we have our ten-year wedding anniversary.

But as adults, I never really got that angry at you. I don't know why. It always seemed like Mark would be okay. I didn't like your friends. But it was fun hanging out with you. Unfortunately your friends were always part of the picture. I tolerated them to get to see my brother. You selected a different lifestyle. I remember being mad that you kept going back to the friends that kept stabbing you in the back. I stayed quiet. I remember mom and dad were always mad at you, the long family nights and speeches. For me it was always seeing you upstairs and talking to the folks again. My advice was the last thing you needed to hear. I didn't want you to get mad at me and reject me since we were finally brothers. That's why I stayed out of your problems. I didn't want to say the same thing that everyone else did. I didn't want to see our relationship crumble. I wanted ours to stay true. I didn't want us to be mad at each other. I don't know if that was the right thing to do. I cherished our time together. Everyone yelled at you. I didn't want our time to be remembered like that. Otherwise, I don't remember you and I talking about all your problems. It was always dad doing the talking upstairs. Then you would come downstairs. We wouldn't talk about your problems. I knew problems were there; we just wouldn't talk about them.

I remember using my artistic talent to get away from it all. The more you were going downhill, the more I forced myself to enter drawing contests and get wrapped up in my art. Kind of crazy times. You had problems and I would win an art contest. We were in opposite directions for a while.

A funny memory I just thought of. Remember when you were living in the town house with a couple guys in Olympia? I think you had just started college, well, for the first time. I must have been 12 years old at the time. You were having a party. That's when we still talked a lot. I called and begged you to take me to the party with you. You bought me non-alcoholic beer. I was a goofball and everyone laughed at me. I wanted to be cool and hang out with you and your friends. We pulled out the hide-a-bed in the living room to go to sleep. You smelled something burning. Somebody left their jacket on the base board heater. Remember the guy came up stairs to leave. He put on his jacket and it had a huge burn mark on the back. We laughed so hard.

Oh, another memory of way back when we were little. We were sleeping in the garage on the hide-a-bed at the house on Cloquallum road. I think it was summer and we were pretending to be camping or something. We came up with these stupid songs. Remember, "hush little baby don't you cry, mommas gonna give you a big black eye." You had to top it though. That was the first time I heard you snort when you laughed. Now I know you do that when ever you laugh real hard. You came up with, "hush little baby don't say a word, mommas gonna lay you a big fat turd. If that turd smells and stinks real bad. Smear it on your face and you'll look real rad!"

Believe it or not out of all this crap I have more fun memories than bad ones. I don't know if that's because the bad ones are blocked out. I don't know. We had fun. We were adopted brothers. We played together. It was really nice too have someone to hang out with. I think of those memories a lot. You know what makes me real happy? We finally get to talk like brothers again and you remember these things too. I never knew that.

I love you, brother.

Royce

Mom and Terry

LIEUTENANT GOVERNOR
BRAD OWEN

Dad and
Linda

Dennis, Dana and Family

Matt and Sherri and Family

Shanie and Peter

Adam and Miranda

Royce, Carrie and Luke

The Whole Gang

XVII

Fictional Reunion With Biological Family

As my life comes full circle to face the very abandonment issues that plagued my life, the next chapter includes working with the adoption support groups. Perhaps my future will include mentoring adopted kids and possibly fielding questions from parents that want to adopt kids. Perhaps one day I will return to Korea to visit the very orphanage where things may have all begun.

In the mean time, I don't know if I'll pursue finding my biological family. I know for now I have started the process to receive closure for these pains. I live believing my fantasy to say hello and goodbye would start something like this:

" Thanking for flying Korean Airways." The stewardess blurped as I rounded the corner from my coach seating to exit the airplane. After 16 hours of non-stop air travel, four meals and not quite enough room to stretch my legs, I was more than ready to exit the stuffy DC12. As I clutched my carry on bag that had my laptop, cell phone, and the new novel I was reading, I replied "Thank you" as my body turned and my eyes drifted downward to make sure the plane and the tarmac were level to each other. I stepped off the plane.

I took long, slow strides down the convoy. It was hot, it was muggy. My pulse was racing and my palms were sweating. 100 million feelings and thoughts racing through my body and soul. After 29 years, I would meet my bio-logical family for the first time. Were my parents tall, short, happy, sad, Korean, Chinese. Do I have brothers and sisters. What about my grandparents? I was almost too anxious to turn the final corner. Would all my lonely and empty days be finally full? Would I have an end to all my years of self-destruction? Would I finally love? Would I finally feel? Would I finally smile?

I made the final corner. The tears streaming from my eyes created a blur that I had to fight through to see. I was overwhelmed with peace, sadness, happiness and emptiness all at the same. It made me cry. I didn't think, I didn't move. It was all slow motion. I panned the faces. Through my eyes, for the first time, I was looking at reflections of myself.

Hi, my name is Lee Yong Yul.........

"God, I offer myself to thee - To build with me and to do with me as though wilt. Relieve me of the bondage of self, that I may better do Thy will. Take away my difficulties, that victory over them may bear witness to those I would help of Thy Power, Thy Love, and Thy Way of Life. May I do Thy will always!"

XVIII

Acknowledgement

The original title for my life story was "Hi, My Name is Lee Yong Yul." The words were followed with a childhood picture of me holding my mother's hand shortly after my adoption and arrival to America. There were several reasons for this title and picture. First, the picture of the small child is how I wanted to remember myself. The small child that felt safe and protected from the evils of this world. The small child living in the age of innocence. The second is how I actually viewed myself. A small, helpless child clinging onto his mother's hand for protection from the evils of this world. A small child who hasn't smiled since the age of 3½ years old.

In recovery, I faced with courage each feeling locked under key within my emotional vault. Each feeling of anger, betrayal, bitterness, helplessness, guilt and shame stemming from my abandonment from my biological family and rejection from an entire Korean culture. I allowed the treatment process to work taking me back to the point the childhood trauma originated, forcing myself to experience the very things that sent me on a lifelong journey medicating my emotional pains through drugs, alcohol and crime. The ultimate numbing whose negative consequences were less painful then the traumas already experienced as a child.

Each negative consequence only reinforced my negative feelings further closing me up and causing hatred towards the world. I hurt others first to not get hurt. I rejected others first to not get rejected. I abandoned others first to never be abandoned again. I pulled people in just to push them away. This was the only sense of control I had in this chaotic, hate filled world I was forced to live in.

In the hours that I felt the most alone and rejected by everyone in the recovery process, I was forced to do the only thing that I had left. I cried for help from the same God that I felt abandoned me as a small child. Streams of endless tears would flow down my face, as I would fall to my hands and knees curling up in a ball on the floor begging God to give me strength. Take away my pain.

There were days I no longer wanted to continue, the emotional pain was to overbearing. But I persevered. I talked to God. I talked to my psychologist. I talked to my counselor. I talked to my housemates. I talked with my sponsor. I talked with my family. I continued with my 12-step recovery program. I trudged forward believing in a greater cause. A greater good.

It's only now in the recovery process that I can look back and see the significance of each situation, each person and each event that was so masterfully placed in my life to bring me back to experience the feelings of gratitude, caring, friendship, respect, honor, trust and love for the first time without the scathed blinders I was wearing.

I pray for those of you that I resented for so long for being the mirror of myself that reflected the hate filled person I was forced to live. I pray that you find the healing from your trauma that only God can provide. The safety and comfort of protective hands that is waiting to return you like me back to your age of innocence.